ULTRATHOUGHTS™ TRIPARTITE

FORBIDDEN PHILOSOPHY

ALTERNATIVE IDEAS ON SCIENCE, RELIGION AND THE GODHEAD

W. DURWOOD JOHNSON

Publisher: Ultrathoughts™ LLC
ultrathoughtsbook@gmail.com
www.ultrathoughts.com

Forbidden Philosophy: Alternative Ideas on Science, Religion and the Godhead

ISBN: 978-1-951731-04-5 (Print)
ISBN: 978-1-951731-05-2 (Ebook)

Library of Congress Control Number: 2019917077
Cover Design by Berge Design

CONTENTS

INSPIRATIONS

Special thanks to few great poetic ultra-thinkers.

Graham Hancock

Nassim Taleb

Leonardo da Vinci

Nikola Tesla

Rupert Sheldrake

Karen Armstrong

Robert J. Shiller

Voltaire

PREFACE

Y ou are the single most important thing in the cosmos, and so is she. With that statement, I have provided you with a tremendous amount of insight into my personal ideology. Pause for a few seconds and really think about that statement. Do you believe it's true? I do. However, I also believe this is a very real delusion I've created within my mind. As a result, the statement can't ever be proven as a manifest truth.

Everyone has a personal ideology or outlook that influences their view of truth, and ultimately, reality. This ideology, a kind of bias outlook, originates from a person's fundamental brain orientation. In the prior books, I referred to my two sisters. They are real people but they are also metaphors for brain hemispheres. The left-leaning older sister represents the left side of the brain that assumes all is logical, material in nature, and quite well-structured. The right-leaning sister represents the other half of the brain. She has a tendency to view the world through a prism colored by creativity, nebulous nature, and flexibility. A truth deemed valid by any individual tends to be framed by thoughts dominated by either the logical or creative side of the brain. Each of my sisters has a particular way of thinking, a pronounced ideological leaning, which tints her world-view.

This third book in a three-volume set is part of my attempt to keep my sisters and society talking. More precisely, it advocates for the creation of deep, contemplative thoughts of a fair mind through a process I call ultra-thinking. When successfully accomplished, it's possible you will produce new and improved ideas, Ultrathoughts. Here in the series finale, I briefly recap the concept of ultra-thinking before presenting over a dozen of my specific Ultrathoughts on topics of science, philosophy, God, and religion.

Throughout the series I have been very honest, probably too honest. Accountants like me don't typically write books about the nature of mind, philosophy, and spirituality unless we conclude neither subject is worthy of serious contemplation. We prefer to focus on themes which lend themselves to facts. Well, that's the leaning of most of us, but every now and then one of us represses our innate nature long enough to truly engage our more creative side. In doing so, we risk offending a few people in the process. I guarantee you I will lose business as a result of daring to put my name on this work. Hey, it's only money; another product of mind. Read my next book, *Money on a Mind*, if you want more on that particular subject.

You may have noticed my style, which my daughter describes as "harsh." I call it efficient. I've worked hard to keep these books short and competently describe some rather dense subject matter in a way that common folk like myself can understand. The point being; there are a number of subjects that people should seriously think about before they fritter their lives away. I urge everyone to take time to put their own opinions to pen and even go so far as to self-publish their own personal book of Ultrathoughts, regardless of education or formal expertise.

A benefit of the process is that it encourages all people to exercise the one trait that makes them special: the ability to deeply contemplate with purpose from both brain hemispheres. I suggest that human beings are inherently kind and loving creatures, but we tend to mature to protect a self which is rooted in personal ideology at the expense of cosmic morality. There is clear evidence that our species is nearing a tipping point. I suggest we may be urging self-extinction by allowing ourselves to be reflexive think-ers. Stop, think, and create better thoughts with intent for the good of you and humanity.

A secondary benefit of the methodology is that it fosters com-munication and understanding between us. We can find common ground once we appreciate our brothers and sisters are doing the best they can to manage their own complicated lives from the prism of their own delusion. Through such understanding maybe we can help reverse societal trends that urge people to literally resent alternative points of view at the expense of enlightenment.

INTRODUCTION

We are each a product of our personal focus. Attention guides the creation of your world, your very reality. The subject of one's attention may be decisively or subconsciously driven; regardless, you will present a person in reflection of your focus. A person who loves money lives in pursuit of money, while a person who loves the Godhead will live for their God. Focus on whatever you like but never deny that the person you present to the world is a product of mind.

I present a person of both intent and happenstance. I try to focus on the righteous but still gawk at a train wreck. Like most, I will probably remain somewhat bound to my historical focus; money, work, the physical pleasures of life, and a particular view of God which was provided to me as a child. Built decades ago, my foundation is well-cured. Nevertheless, I seem to have expanded my views creating a sort of revised philosophy. The revision has brought me a certain peace of mind. Ultra-thinking has worked for me personally.

Before we get into my "forbidden philosophy," my revised views of truth, I wish to take a moment to provide you with some background. This will add context that will help you appreciate that while the topics might appear random, each is an important chapter in the narrative of my mind. Without this background we may part with you left wondering: is he serious?

Repeatedly, I have self-confessed my bias: a left-brained leaning, overtly-rational thinker. Furthermore, I've mentioned I have two sisters and am very similar to my left-leaning sister. Though they tend to avoid serious topics, when my sisters have those rare substantive discussions, an argument often ensues. Being a classical middle child, I step in and try to make peace. Although my head is usually in agreement with the sister who seems to be more rational, I often feel the need to defend the creative sister out of pity. My immediate reaction to many of her views is to consider them rather ill-conceived so she probably needs my help.

For decades when my right-brain oriented sister spoke with me in retort, I had serious doubts as to whether she had even heard what I was saying. She appeared to flat out ignore me. Getting overly-excited about my very rational answers, I assumed she spoke out from a position of pure emotion. I simply couldn't fathom her response and rarely paused to seriously consider her view. My innate bias told me she must be shutting off her brain when she got upset. I heard what she said. She was wrong; end of story.

Still I was puzzled. I know she's very intelligent; she has a couple of degrees. Her temperament is stable; mild if anything. She has a fine career and with her husband, she's raising four scholarly children. She had to understand what I said and my logic certainly seemed flawless. Was she living in some alternative reality or was I really that cold calculating beast she seems to think I am? After all, my daughter does call me harsh and my tone does often sound condescending. Fortunately, there is a proxy to observe in my stead: the extremely rational and logical left-brain-oriented sister.

Stepping back and listening to each speak, or argue, I was able to view the action as an observer. This gave me a hint of neutrality that I would never have had as a participant in the discussion. I noticed they each tended to approach a topic from completely different sides. I eventually came to appreciate that my right-brain-oriented sister was thinking through her answers intelligently, but her fundamental ideology is so different from the older sister that the younger's well-conceived ideas were heard as irrational silliness. The left-brainer reflexively dismissed the right-brainer, hearing her words as emotional outbursts. The younger sister did something similar but in reverse. She automatically dismissed any argument she heard which seemed to be rooted in pure unforgiving logic. The words of the older sister were quickly dismissed as being the harsh ravings of a mean-spirited person. Though the younger sister did so with less condescending flair, they equally disrespected the views of the other.

They failed to resolve conflicts because they didn't bother to understand a fundamental facet of the mind: ideology guides your mind-myth narrative to automatically shut out alternative ideas. It's one's own mind that determines truth and mind favors its historical view far more than an enlightened perspective. My two sisters might as well be speaking different languages, and unless or until they recognized they each harbor a seriously biased outlook, the entire discussion was a waste of energy and the argument would continue until one simply stomped away.

Even with this explanation offered, few would believe an accountant would write about mind, truth, and meta concepts. An evaluation of such nebulous topics rarely comes from the mind of an overtly-rational thinker. The difference in my case is my obsessive nature. I wasn't content to simply appreciate what was happening between my sisters, I needed to dive deeper and understand how anyone could create a new truth.

A critical hurdle to clear in my self-enlightenment journey was to accept that interpretations of my experiences are far more important to me personally than the actual substance of matter. True, physical "stuff" is important but absent my cognition of the physical its relevance to me is debatable. Ideas of mind, ideas having no basis in physical reality, dominate my relevant truths and from that perspective I create my own type of reality. Such view runs counter to my innately logical leanings, but this is now my truth. The phrase "think it to be it" is a succinct way to express the dominance of mind over matter. The meta, spiritual, or non-physical realm is master over the physical. This is one of the first themes presented in the set of books collectively called the Ultrathoughts Tripartite.

It took more than two decades of ultra-thinking for me to appreciate that my mind creates and protects my ideologically-driven truth. I have since concluded that each and every person on the planet is actually somewhat off-kilter. After all, we each live a delusion. Therefore, the only relevant question is at what point does a person's self-created delusion fall so far outside that of society that he or she should be considered mad. I don't consider myself mad, but you may believe I'm pushing my luck.

Ultrathoughts are the product of forcing the mind to do something I call ultra-thinking. Ultra-thinking is a process of creating deep contemplative thoughts while suppressing your ideology. To ultra-think productively, one must force themselves to use both the logical-left and creative-right hemispheres of the brain. This means the thinker must at least temporarily respect alternative facts. Any and all points of view must be given credibility within the mind. This process, a type of whole-brain thinking, is far more difficult than it sounds due to our tendency to surround ourselves with people who reinforce our own ideology.

We each have an ideology that becomes intertwined with our personal narrative or mind-myth. To question your mind-myth is to doubt the person you have created. Most of us don't readily seek to question our core beliefs. Yet, if you don't earnestly challenge your own automatic beliefs occasionally, the person you become will likely be an ill-informed reflection of your leaning.

I'm not purporting to question your specific ideology or personal beliefs. I am, however, questioning the wisdom of allowing yourself to become a purely reflexive thinker immersed in ideology. The ultra-thinking premise assumes it is best to think from a fair and balanced mind. When successfully accomplished, ultra-thinking will create not only better ideas but an improved or refined version of your delusional truth. To ultra-think is to exercise your innate ability to think like no other creature on the planet today. To deny this instinct is to disrespect our species. The ancients understood the value of thought, and in these books, I promote the same wisdom.

Book one, *Intentional Thought*, explained the process of ultra-thinking and its product, Ultrathoughts, in some detail. In the book, I urged every member of society to attempt to find common ground with others. Seek out those who fundamentally challenge your view of the world in hopes of improving yourself. This concept doesn't mean to imply your existing view is categorically wrong, only that your current truth is likely to be a reflexive view. Ultra-thinking simply seeks to expand your outlook by restraining your historical or innate bias to think a fresh thought. Certainly, reconsideration may not always bring about a change of mind. Regardless, the process is worthy because at a minimum ultra-thinking will help bring about clarity, which will result in confidence of belief.

The case for acceptance of my premise was bolstered in book two, *Godhead Designs*. I told you about my personal history, my drama if you will, in an attempt to expose my bias nature to you. I don't want anything I write to be considered a promotion of one god-view over another. Evangelism or advocacy of any design is not my thing. As you will soon read, I have very specific views but actually don't recommend them to anybody. Progressing through book two we clarified some definitions of terms like *god* and *soul*. Without having a consistent understanding of terms, we can't have a productive discussion about these subjects. I then summarized what we believe the ancient Egyptians thought in general. Although no one living for the past couple of millennia can truly know what the ancients thought, we did our best to try and appreciate their perspective. In the style expected by a left-brainer like your author, we progressively worked through the evolution of Godhead philosophies starting with Pythagoras and ending with René Descartes. Recognizing that nearly eighty-five percent of the world is religious and well over three-quarters of those identify their spiritual God as basically a version of the One God of Abraham, we devoted much of our attention to a consideration of monotheism—particularly that centered on the Christian religion.

I appreciate that we are covering a tremendous amount of material in the series. These are heavy subjects to consider, particularly if you are not accustomed to thinking about important issues that go to your core. As you've read, I believe we each create our truth within our minds. That creation is either a conscious or subconscious choice. Ultimately, you will find your truth whether you intend to or not. That truth just seems to be there in the end. I suggest you seek to guide your truth with intention.

Ultra-thinking is what I wish to promote, not my own dogma or truth. The Old Hippie and Old General types (described in book one of the series) will scoff at my idea that we each have our reality, not just our own truths. They would have little interest in exploring or admitting their bias. You do not. You appreciate that reality is all that matters when we strip everything else away, and you prefer to have an optimal reality. To create the optimal, sometimes one must reconstruct. My concept of ultra-thinking questions a closed-minded version of the truth and suggests our truths should often be reconsidered.

To be fearless in thought creation one must not be intimidated by subjects that seem esoteric or incomprehensible. Such themes shouldn't be avoided; they should be sought. Ultrathoughts Tripartite has been a trying project. It is patently-obvious that I am not a professional writer, philosopher, scientist, or theologian. To get through this process, I constantly reminded myself that what made great thinkers special was a willingness to consider the outrageous and go on record with their fair-minded conclusions. With self-awareness and a touch of humility, most can write their own narrative with intent. If you write well enough, your ideas may present a poetic truth which stands the test of time. Having the work of sculptor Auguste Rodin in mind, I suggest The Thinker is transformed back to The Poet as he or she was meant to be. If I've confused you with that last statement; Google his most famous statue and ponder the Ultrathoughts™ logo.

This will seem strange, but my heart aches for some of my more dogmatic friends and family. The series was not written for them. I hope I'm wrong, but I fear they're too far gone to seek enlightenment preferring the comfortable embrace of a reflexive self. These books are written for you and my legacy. You aren't a lost cause. If you try to ultra-think and actively seek to suppress your own dogma long enough to create Ultrathoughts, you will be a better person. You can think intentional thoughts and continually seek whole-brain enlightenment as you find common ground with those who think differently.

What follows is the finale, *Forbidden Philosophy*. The book is based solely on my own delusion. I give credit to all thinkers who have thought before because I honestly don't know if all, few, or none of my Ultrathoughts are original. I'm inclined to believe there are few, if any, original thoughts. *Homo sapiens* and hominins in general have been around for an awfully long time, so it is possible all thoughts have been thought before. From my reading and study, it seems to me that even the great masterminds of old weren't afraid to simply rework ideas passed on from predecessors. I often wonder if there's some sort of cosmic transmission of common wisdom. Regardless, my version of reality and truth is what follows. You're welcome to take or assign credit as you deem appropriate. My truth, wisdom, and indeed my words are fleeting in the end anyway.

These words, presented in the digital ether and cataloged, shall live long after the physical individual has returned to dust. If the stars align just right, maybe the concept of ultra-thinking will prove to be a catalyst for action. More people may actively seek to restrain themselves from their own ideological leaning and ultra-think in the process. My premier Ultrathought is that whole-brain, fair-minded thinking, fostered in a mind that suppresses one's personal dogma or ideological leaning, will benefit humanity. Mine has a twist in emphasis, but in many ways the Ultrathought is a spin on the ideas of Plato. If my tripartite of books spur you to ultra-think, then Plato, you and I share this truth. If not, I still believe the world has been improved by your consideration of the premise. To think is good for humanity even if we don't agree in the end. Here I present my truth, my delusion; a forbidden philosophy is revealed.

Part I

CHAPTER 1

ULTRATHOUGHTS OF SCIENCE

O ne of the most important aspects of ultra-thinking is to be fearless in your thoughts and not be intimidated by any subject. Socrates had no PhD, yet he is credited as the father of all of Western philosophy. Have no shame in revealing your own silly ideas, for the plain fact is that today's dream is tomorrow's visionary truth. As we mature, a leaning can come to dominate the mind-myth and produce ideologically-tinted answers to life's questions. Have you ever noticed some of the most insightful responses come from children? That is a direct result of their having a rather thin ideological cloud hanging over their judgment. They express from innate brain power without a reality filter created by society and thought narratives fed them by educators. As we approach the following subjects, keep this in mind: Leonardo da Vinci had little or no formal education yet he is considered one of the greatest thinkers of all time.

If you have no technical training but are an intelligent and thinking being, you can contemplate the world's weighty subjects. Have absolutely no fear or shame in considering life's questions. It is your right to think and it's all a delusion anyway.

Having no technical training in science, I will not attempt to provide much background on these subjects. I'm confident I understand them enough to ultra-think, but any of the following topics in this section are worth a lifetime of study, and it is entirely possible I may have misunderstood certain key points. However, this is a work of my mind; not scientific rigor. I encourage you to read, review, investigate, and create your own truth with intent.

Part one exposes my forbidden and quite possibly ill-conceived notions related to science. I hope you are challenged enough to disagree, because then you will be on your way to ultra-thinking your own truth.

CHAPTER 2

LIFE-FORCE AND ENTANGLEMENT

When we consider a topic like life, let's start by first admitting that our best and brightest minds of science can't unequivocally describe what life actually is. This may surprise you, but it is absolutely true. The definition of life has continued to ebb and flow since humans first contemplated their existence, possibly hundreds of thousands of years ago. Regardless, we need to define the term. For our purposes, we'll define *life* as meaning strictly organic or biological life. Life is then ascribed to any carbon-based organism that has the capacity to grow, metabolize, reproduce, adapt, and respond.

All living organisms are comprised of matter ultimately created by molecules comprised of atoms. As you may know, atoms are never perfectly still. They vibrate or exist in a state of Brownian motion. This vibration causes the atoms to give off tiny, but measurable, amounts of energy. Not only do they continuously give off energy, but they store energy in the form of nuclear energy. This store of nuclear energy can be tapped—but not easily. As you're probably aware, the splitting of a single uranium-235 atom releases an incredible amount of stored energy. This instant release of energy produced the first atomic bomb. What you may not recognize is that, theoretically, the splitting of any atom would release an incredible amount of energy. In summary, all atoms give off and store energy.

Concerning the energy stored in our particular organism, the human body, we are made up of about seven billion billion billion atoms. That is seven followed by twenty-seven zeros. These are organized to form the elements or compounds of our living body. If these atoms were split and their energy was harnessed, one human's worth of energy would provide enough power to run a large city for years. Let this fact of physics settle in your mind. One body could power a city for years, assuming we could effectively harness the energy within the atoms!

When any living organism dies, those atoms remain; however, they deteriorate to be organized differently. The fundamental building blocks of life, carbon-based atoms, return to their rather disorganized state. They may, for various reasons, reorganize over time, but there is apparently no particular need for this to happen. The atoms that were once a fern or a snail one billion years ago may tomorrow become part of your pet poodle. At this very moment you may even be made up of millions of the exact same atoms that were at some point part of a Tyrannosaurs Rex named Sue or Queen Cleopatra of ancient Egypt.

To put this dynamic in terms of ancient Stoic philosophy, the "stuff of life" returns to physical matter, also known as the stuff of God. Or, as many cosmologists would say, the physical matter of life, at death, returns to the stuff of stars—carbon. The Stoics certainly have a point, but this can't be the whole story.

Biological life is unique amongst other collections of atoms. Unlike the atoms that make up a rock or a smartphone, the organized atoms of life produce unique energy. Biological life generates a particular energy from a process called cellular respiration. This energy is expressed only by atoms organized as a living creature. The expression occurs as the creature metabolizes the fuel necessary for its existence. This energy can be measured. The measurement is challenging but doable.

Nevertheless, time and time again the numbers don't add up. Something else is apparently happening. When measurements are made, there is more energy produced by life than can be explained through cellular respiration. Is this unexplainable surplus energy a simple miscalculation, or are scientists being shown specifically that there is another force of energy beyond that which we know?

Regarding this particular challenge, it appears the best idea scientists have come up with is to represent that any measured surplus is most likely simple random variation. Unfortunately, their best guess has some major problems, the most blatant being that these supposed random fluctuations can be manipulated. If these were truly random, of course, they could not be influenced with purpose. The second and bigger challenge is the amount of surplus energy. The variances can be huge. The actual energy amount over that predicted is so large as to call into question the formulas themselves. As an analogy, let's say you have calculated the amount of energy it takes to boil an egg. All's going fairly-well as you boil and calculate the amount of electricity used to boil five individual eggs. Then, all of a sudden, the sixth egg takes fifty times the amount of energy to boil. If this happens once, you might overlook it, but if it happens every sixth egg, either the fundamental model is wrong or there is something else happening.

Concerning the unexplained energy of life most traditional scientists prefer neither option, so they simply ignore the mystery. Fortunately considerations of this strange, ill-defined energy of life have been deemed a worthy topic by dogma-restrained alternative scientists who dare to explore the metaphysical. Many refer to this inexplicable energy of life as *life force energy*. Just to clarify, cellular respiration is a predictable amount of energy produced by a living organism. The energy beyond that of cellular respiration is the energy we are referring to here. Life force energy is energy of a meta or nonphysical nature, while cellular respiration energy is a physically based expression of effort.

While life force energy currently defies reasonable explanation, the energy is measurable and can't be denied. This particular topic often morphs into discussions concerning other types of mysterious energy. You may have heard some speak of universal energy, collective consciousness energy, "the field," or even zero-point energy. Many are inclined to believe all of these energies are either one with, or directly related to, the surplus living energy—life force energy.

I've spent a number of years ultra-thinking this topic and wish to relate the issue to a particular phenomenon of quantum physics. What I find most fascinating about life force energy is its fluctuation. Why does it change, and is this change purposeful?

It has long been accepted by hundreds if not thousands of doctors that, in ways science can't explain, thoughts influence outcomes experienced by others. Thoughts—call them prayers, if you wish—may one day be proven beyond doubt to influence measurable energy. If we assume the energy of life is a meta energy and the effects of thoughts are also meta in nature, then we might infer a spiritual event. If thoughts and prayers do in fact influence a physical being, they are doing so indirectly via the forced expression of a meta event.

Through my own investigative study of spiritual philosophy and the consideration of the Ultrathoughts of various intellectual giants, it has become evident to me that this life-force-related extra energy field documents a unique aspect of life. This energy is quite possibly related to the spiritual realm.

Experiments have shown that a healthy organism expresses more vibrant energy than an unhealthy one. A vibrant field is not only more expressive, but it has also been shown to be more receptive to influence. In other words, a vibrant healthy organism is one whose life is engaged with the fields of other living creatures. A duller field, on the other hand, is not so engaged.

Many living organisms may one day be proven to successfully use the meta realm with intent to produce an influence on others. While we know for a fact that the sight of your dog's wagging tail invokes a physical reaction in you, is it possible that at least some of this reaction is the result of meta rather than physical stimuli? Is it possible that your pet is mentally projecting some type of energy influence to move you to provide her with a treat? When you feel the need to run home and walk the dog, are you doing so because you want to or because the dog is communicating a need?

It is possible that all living creatures influence each other to one degree or another. Heretofore, most have assumed humans are the masters of manipulation. We use physical and psychological means with intent to get what we want. However, we understand very little about our own mind and virtually nothing about the minds of other animals. Even a dog might to one extent or another manipulate its energy field in a manner that influences that of its master. Could a dolphin use a meta energy field to interact with a whale for some unknown purpose? Could a school of mackerel acting in unison with amazing speed be using energy fields or life force energy as a means of communicating?

If that isn't wild enough, other experiments seem to prove there is an interaction between life force energies, regardless of conscious awareness or intent. There are respectable and repeatable experiments showing that a person's energy field measurably changes when in the presence of his or her child or important pet. Such measurable events have been shown to occur even if the person has no conscious awareness of the presence. In such conditions, the test subject can't be reacting to any stimuli known to our five senses: touch, smell, sight, sound, and taste. Many who seek to refute the results are confident that, subconsciously, subjects are reacting to environmental stimuli too subtle to be noticed by the experimenter. However, highly-controlled experiments lend support to the idea that through a yet unknown channel, living organisms, cells, or atoms are interacting. This force, a metaphysical force, operates outside the laws of physics and may be connected to what we've called life force energy.

While many researchers over the past few decades have concentrated on the life force energy, which can be measured to a distance of twenty-five or so feet, others have pushed the boundaries further. Newer experiments seem to confirm that certain living organisms remain connected regardless of distance. If confirmed, these newer experiments would obviously disprove the idea that subjects are picking up on subtle, yet physical, stimuli. Twins, spouses, and siblings separated by oceans can't be aware of each other's presence through a subtle smell or noise.

I need to pause here and briefly explain a very odd but well-documented curiosity of quantum mechanics: quantum entanglement. Without boring or confusing you, entanglement is a physical property that occurs when pairs of subatomic and possibly atomic particles remain related despite separation. The state of being of each can't be explained independently regardless of the distance between them. Offered purely as a metaphor, let's say we each have a television. You're in London and I'm on the planet Pluto. At the moment you change the channel, mine changes with absolutely no delay. The televisions are entangled. Quantum entanglement experiments prove that particles like electrons, and possibly far larger particles, remain related in an explicable manner.

Researchers studying the influence of one life on another appear to be showing something very similar to quantum entanglement regarding living organisms. Twins, spouses, siblings, or even you and your pet cat, may one day be proven to be entangled.

As I stated, quantum entanglement is said to be a physical property. This seems rather odd given the fact that the communication between entangled particles is instantaneous. Don't gloss over that word—instantaneous. Experiments document that related particles are somehow influencing each other without the passing of any measurable pocket of time! That, in my mind, means this is no physical property. Entanglement is a meta property, not a physical property.

In ultra-thinking the idea that certain living organisms or even persons may be entangled, I'm led to consider the means of communication. Those thoughts bring me to the issue of universal energy and the idea that maybe the entire cosmos is connected. If universal connectivity served as a kind of network existing outside the constraints of the physical realm, then certainly communication would be instantaneous.

Ultra-thinking topics like life force energy and the idea that some, if not all, of us are entangled naturally morphs into considerations of prayer. An honest evaluation of several controlled scientific experiments concerning the benefit of positive thinking or prayer lends ample support for the conclusion that prayer actually works. We don't understand how, but if a person literally focuses without distraction or the counter-influence of noisy energy, the focuser oftentimes can influence a living organism.

My favorite examples of these types of events are ones in which groups of individuals, who may not even know they are part of a group, act with intent to bring about healing or change, and the subject experiences a benefit. In fairness, because the results are not always quantifiable or repeatable, thoughts and prayers are not deemed a worthy course of medical treatment. That said, I say with complete confidence that if you ask a medical doctor, many will admit that although they don't understand how, their personal experience leads them to conclude that prayer can actually work.

My Ultrathoughts conclude that there is some sort of specialness to life that defies any physical explanation to date. The unique nature of living organized matter might provide a clue to the existence and operating characteristics of the spiritual realm. Living organisms may have the ability to manipulate their own life force energy, and in certain cases, by manipulating their own energy, organisms might exert an influence on other life. The instantaneous nature of this communication implies some type of meta network.

CHAPTER 3

SUPERPOSITION IN RELATION TO REALITY

The superposition of all possible states, or the wave function, deals with the nature of physical reality within the context of a branch of science called quantum physics. This particular concept deals with the actual state of being of atomic or subatomic particles. When we say "all possible states," we are considering an instance wherein the object is expressed through a statistically weighted mathematical formula (wave function) as being present in all possible states at the same time. I would like to offer an example to serve as a metaphor, but don't misunderstand—this is a metaphor only.

Assuming the state of being for a water molecule, H_2O, could be expressed simultaneously as solid ice, liquid water, and water vapor, we could say that the H_2O molecule is in a superposition of all possible states—not one or the other state, nor the average of the three possibilities—all at the same time, simultaneously expressed through a weighted mathematical formula. Should you wish to investigate this subject on your own, be aware that when we consider superposition, we are also dealing with topics like the wave function, interference patterns, and quantum entanglement. None of these topics are fully understood, even by the individuals who write the theories, so you should not feel discouraged if you are a bit overwhelmed. For our purposes, we'll stop and summarize by simply saying a superposition is a state of being in itself and does occur.

Many believe this is a statement of clear fact that can be accepted unequivocally, but others believe this state of being, superposition, is unique to considerations of the quantum (small things)—that this concept would only apply to particles like electrons, photons, and the components that make up larger particles like neutrons. However, there is a growing volume of scientific research supporting the conclusion that this strange quantum property is also relevant to much larger particles. Some believe that even groups of atoms, which may comprise actual molecules, can also exist in a superposition of all possible states.

Now let's move on to another subject I will be relating to superposition: decoherence. There is no need to overcomplicate this concept. Coherence is more or less synonymous with togetherness. Decoherence is the negative of coherence: a state of transition from stability to another state. Decoherence within the context of quantum physics is far more nuanced than I am presenting, but I'm confident you'll get the gist of it. What is important for you to appreciate is that, as far as we can tell, quantum physics has proven that decoherence can be brought about by observation. Pause and think about that statement. Observation apparently brings about a state of change - decoherence.

Returning to the metaphorical example of H_2O, let's assume you are on the verge of observing a molecule of water currently in a superposition of all possible states. The water is in neither a state of ice, liquid, or vapor, being currently in this weird quasi-state. Through simple observation, glancing at the molecule in a microscope, you bring on decoherence out of superposition toward a specific state that is now static—ice, for example. Observation is the specific action that moves the H_2O from superposition (all states at once) to a specific state of being.

If that's not strange enough, the manifested state, ice in our example, is the state you specifically chose. Reread the statement if you like, but you understood correctly. The result of the observer's *desire* was foretold by the observed molecule of water. In tortured language, reality is "real" before it can be appreciated.

In support of this concept, physicists have confirmed that when they perform a general experiment called the double-slit experiment, a photon of light expresses the characteristics of both a wave and particle. The photon, unobserved, is then in superposition. Further experimentation shows that specific experiments that attempt precise measurement of a photon of light as a particle inexplicably bring out the desired manifest state: particle. The converse is true when scientists measure or observe the photon as a wave. Measurement brings about decoherence, and the observer somehow invokes the state desired. The smartest minds in our world don't understand why this occurs or necessarily what qualifies as observation regarding decoherence, but quantum physics accepts the situation described above.

Now we'll move forward to discuss a third facet of the quantum world, conservation. Once a particle, say a light photon, fixes a specific state of being, that photon resists changing to another state. Using our example, H_2O as ice resists changing from ice to water. Change takes effort. Within the context of physics, laws of conservation tell us that once a particle is in a state, it tends to stay in that same state absent outside force. Furthermore, the bigger the particle the more effort is required to change its state. Larger things are extremely unlikely to change. We could say that generally larger particles are fixed and smaller particles are less fixed. This property of conservation is a tendency, not a hard and fast rule, which is why particles like electrons occasionally suddenly disappear and simultaneously reappear in another state and location. With that point admitted, the fact remains; what is "real" tends to stay as it is.

To round out our discussion, superposition is the state of being all possible states. Decoherence is dis-organization. Conservation is the tendency of a given state of being to stay constant. I provide this background as a foundation for an Ultrathought.

There is an idea that decoherence itself is not brought about so much by observation but by the interaction of one thing with another. Interaction could be the critical feature of decoherence, not an intentional observation or measurement.

My ultra-thinking considers that it stands to reason that the more interaction a particle has with more "stuff," the stronger the principle of conservation. Just as conservation or stability of a state can be stronger or weaker based on size, the influence of decoherence could be stronger or weaker. Again, back to the water example, if one specific observer influenced a water molecule to move from superposition to the specific state of ice, that state of being—ice—would be stable. It then stands to reason that if not one but one hundred thousand observers brought about the decoherence simultaneously, then the resulting ice could be in a more stable state than if that same ice had been manifested because of a single observation.

Now let's expand the concept from the metaphor to a photon of light. If a light photon interacted with an entire planet instead of with one simple atom, the property of coherence or stability in the observed state of being will be stronger. Within the context of physics, coherence is strongest when waves share what's called a constant phase difference. When this is strong, the stability of the state is strong; when weak, decoherence to a new state is more likely. More observations or possibly more interactions with more atoms increases the strength of conservation, while fewer interactions make decoherence more likely.

I want to make it clear that with the above statement, my personal Ultrathought, we've moved into pure conjecture, which is not a scientific hypothesis to my knowledge. My Ultrathought is based partially on my appreciation of a truly strange but well-documented peculiarity of the quantum.

Experiments lend support to the hypothesis that any object could disappear and simultaneously reappear in a different location. You understood that sentence correctly; the name of this principle is the Heisenberg uncertainty principle. To clarify, this is not a movement from point A to point B. The principle is similar in concept to quantum entanglement. The "popping" in or out of physical presence is instantaneous. Not only have observations confirmed that this actually happens for subatomic particles like electrons, but recent experiments appear to confirm the same phenomenon is observable for matter the size of fifty molecules. The mathematics behind the principle support the idea that this is possible for objects of any size. Put plainly, in theory, any sized object can simply pop in and out of existence.

Imagine your car vanishing from your driveway and simultaneously appearing in your neighbor's kitchen. As strange as this sounds, quantum science tells us this is possible at any point in time. The number of subatomic interactions that would have to happen in unison to make it occur may involve statistical improbabilities, like one in a billion squared, but it could happen. Still, for very small things, the odds are substantially reduced. So instead of a car, let us consider a microscopic grain of sand doing the same vanishing act. The odds of this microscopic rock appearing out of nowhere are still incredibly remote, say one in a hundred million, but they are drastically improved; not a billion squared.

Of course, no one would ever see the vanishing car or grain of sand. However, what if our particle was a million times smaller than a grain of sand? Does it stand to reason that these spontaneous events may occur often but don't occur for anything other than incredibly small particles? Yes, that is exactly what happens.

Analysis of the quantum provides support for theories which document that particles literally pop out and back into our material reality simultaneously.

As if this entire discussion isn't strange enough, I would like to build on my ultra-thinking and relate the concept to the spiritual realm. Let's assume for a moment that the immaterial soul of a person is indeed partnered with the material physical body. This soul is a spiritual entity, for lack of a better description.

Being meta, the soul exists without atoms or mass. The spiritual soul is partnered with a physical living person, but the soul is not expressed in any particular state of being; the soul is in a sort of superposition. A soul could then be described as being in a state similar to a photon of light, unless and until that soul is observed. Could we then say the physical body can bring about the decoherence of the soul if the physical person "seeks," or observes that soul? Maybe it is more proper to say that the soul would not move to true decoherence (the soul itself having no matter) but would still be subject to the unsettling stress of potential decoherence as the living body interacts with the soul.

Along this same line of ultra-thinking, we can then consider the question of degree of influence a physical body would have on his or her soul. Doesn't it stand to reason that the more materially-oriented a person is, or the more interaction a person has with matter impacting the soul, the more the influence of not only decoherence but the force of conservation on the soul?

Recall that in my initial premise the soul is immaterial and spiritual, existing in its own unique kind of superposition. As I interact with the physical world, taking my soul along for the ride, my soul is subject to influence. My soul is influenced toward a different state of being. I put upon my soul through my interactions in the material realm. We could then say a soul, partnered with a body, has a tendency toward a state of being rather than a superposition of all possible states.

Now recall the idea of conservation, which informs us that once a state is set, further change is resisted. Once a soul is partnered with a body it's influenced out of its natural state of superposition to fix in a specific physical state. Fixed in a new state the soul would find it difficult to return to its natural state. In short, the physical body influences my soul to stabilized in a state of being that is offensive to its preferred state of superposition. A material reality puts upon a soul. My body, therefore, "contaminates" my soul automatically. This is the very definition of original sin in my view. Each individual whether or not they act with intent will put upon their soul.

In conclusion, let me remind you that various ancient spiritual texts refer to the afterlife challenge of any "rich" man. A rich (i.e., materially engulfed) person's soul will find it virtually impossible to reach "heaven". This ancient wisdom may have been simply presenting the following Ultrathought: The more physical interaction the person has with the stuff of material matter, the harder it is for his or her soul to return to its natural (superposition-like) state, a heavenly state of bliss.

CHAPTER 4

THE QUANTUM WAVE FUNCTION AND MIRACLES

To assign time and space is to observe, forcing decoherence on the subatomic particle. This brings about a manifestation of physical reality, a state of being. Once observed, the target object is forced to behave like a particle; when not observed, the object is expressed in the math of the statistically weighted wave function.

While the act of observation brings about a specific reality, that specific reality is predictable to a degree of certainty. What we experience as a specific physical reality is the manifestation of these statistical probabilities, which can be modeled as a formula. From any given formula of prediction a statistical likelihood can be calculated.

In our daily experience, what is statistically likely is what we understand as physical reality. The physical presence of your car staying in your driveway can be reduced to a mathematical calculation of statistical likelihood. Mathematical models can show that your car will remain at its location to a degree of certainty. For example, the formula may predict that, statistically speaking, your car would stay at its present location for a trillion earth years on average absent force or deterioration. The point is - the probability that your car will stay put is never going to be one hundred percent certain. Still, from a statistical standpoint, once you go beyond odds of a billion to one we could say your car *will* stay.

Now think of that car appearing in your neighbor's kitchen. From your own practical experience, your mind-myth doesn't consider this plausible or even a possibility. Mathematically it's not impossible, but in the history of humanity, no car has ever spontaneously appeared in a kitchen. So, regarding one's created narrative, the likelihood of an event occurring is deemed impossible. For all practical purposes, the event lies outside our reality. This issue was previously discussed in book one, *Intentional Thought*, as we explored the carnival balloon of reality, but I need to stress the point in forming a foundation for further Ultrathoughts.

What makes up your entire delusion is only that deemed relevant to you. If you don't care or are simply too dull to think, your entire reality is left to your mind's interpretation of information received from your physical senses. I doubt a sponge has much of a mind-myth or a resulting reality. The human mind is more. We are rational, but we aren't computers. Our mind makes judgments of worthiness, not mathematical calculations. Reality, or the truth of your mind, is a product of both deduction and faith however, neither matters unless the thinker considers the subject worth thinking about. We must care to create. The self-created story can only be true when you first deem something relevant and plausible. Back to the carnival balloon visual. Plausibility, a simple consideration by the mind, determines whether your truth will include any idea within its balloon.

If I have denied any possibility of a car appearing spontaneously, and then actually observe the event, I would say this was a miracle. It was not possible in my mind. Such an event is inexplicable and had been previously denied in my reality.

Now that I've informed you that quantum considerations appreciate any car appearance at any moment in time is a possibility, you probably still wouldn't consider such an event an objectively proven fact supported by science. The event is simply so implausible that it is still deemed literally impossible by the mind despite the fact it is theoretically possible. Plausibility trumps possibility within your mind.

On the other hand, had I accepted the idea as both possible and plausible I would consider the appearance of the car as confirmation of my existing interpretation of physical reality. The spontaneous appearance of a car was unexpected, but because I believed it was plausible in my enlightened estimation, this prevented me from attributing any actual appearance to the status of a miracle. My enlightened truth was impactful of my very reality. I had knowledge of physical reality having been informed of the possibility of said event, and its observation merely confirmed the unusual yet "true" experience.

Mind is dominant in defining reality. A mind which assumes all is physical sees no miracles, merely unexplained physical phenomena. Implied in the statement is a connection between miracles and the unexplainable nature of the meta realm. I suggest a person's interpretation of a miracle is dependent on one's own overall view of reality. The "sight" of a miracle is reasonable if your own delusional reality has accepted the spiritual realm in contemplation. It is not reasonable if you deny the plausibility of any inexplicable events, ever. In rejecting any plausibility of a meta event you implicitly view any unexplained event as a temporary lack of knowledge or a simple misreading of the situation at hand. Believers will believe, and those who don't will deny any prospect of a meta event. Each will be equally confident in their opinion.

To one who takes the spiritual realm as a given, miracles themselves are plausible with or without any rational foundation. Any belief in such a miracle observed is supported within the mind by a belief that an inexplicable realm exists. Believers in the spiritual are therefore more likely to see miracles because they have trained the mind to expect the inexplicable from time to time.

My Ultrathought is a basic understanding that the quantum wave function provides support for a belief in an inexplicable realm. The wave function provides theoretical math that may continue to be confirmed through the application of quantum mechanics. Of course, it may also be proven to be an utter misunderstanding of math or observation. To a believer in miracles, the reason is unimportant.

When ultra-thinking subjects like spontaneous miracles that seem to defy the laws of physics, one must resist the tendency to stay grounded in our preconception of what is a physical reality. Physical reality may appear certain and in some cases is supported by objective mathematical models, but technically it is in no way certain. Neither math nor science dictate reality. They may infer a particular story or mind-myth of reality, but they set no standards themselves. It is the mind that determines your truth. Don't misunderstand—it's not likely a car will appear in your kitchen, and I will categorically say it won't in common discussion. However, framing such consideration within a discussion of the very nature of my reality, yes, I'm saying there's always a chance.

CHAPTER 5

ELECTROMAGNETISM, BRAIN, AND REALITY

The strong force and electromagnetism hold the particles of an atom and molecule together. In a sense, these forces represent an act or influence. I suggest they're participating in a kind of mutual observation that brings about a state of being for physical atoms. That state is a fixed state subject to the laws of conservation. The atoms and molecules we experience are our physical reality because they bothered to engage and observe.

Let's assume a similar dynamic is happening with regard to the spiritual realm. Like physical matter, the spiritual has a default state of being. This default state is different from that of the physical. The default position of the spiritual is a superposition of all possible states. Being a kind of state, the laws of conservation still apply and decoherence is resisted.

The spiritual realm seeks to remain in a superposition of all states, and any force that influences otherwise is therefore anti-spiritual. The forces of electromagnetism or any similar forces represent an anti-spiritual influence.

The human brain and any living organism made of physical matter can be influenced by these same natural forces: the strong force and electromagnetism. The latest research in brain science using electromagnetism has even reported that through manipulation of this energy, target subjects can experience relief of symptoms associated with post-traumatic stress. Researchers don't understand why it happens, but improvement can be seen in test subjects.

In another shocking surprise, the latest research in brain energy supports a hypothesis that although brain energy fields themselves are incredibly weak, the brain is capable of using its field for communication. By using brain energy instead of synaptic cellular connections, the brain acts more like a quantum computer changing on the fly without the passing of a moment in time as opposed to the way we've conventionally thought of the brain. Traditionally, science has taught us to think of the brain as a bundle of neurocellular connections, but this entire paradigm may change in the very near future. Given the extremely weak nature of brain energy, one would assume this energy would be unusually susceptible to the influence of electromagnetism. Does this influence hinder the brain in its development and construction of mind-myth?

Let's assume the mind of a human exists because of an action by the brain in one manner or another. It is certainly possible that electromagnetism, fundamental to all matter, is somehow interacting with the brain's own field. Further research might one day provide an indication of our unique abilities, which in turn could lead us to note a special spiritual nature to the human living organism.

With deference to the mind-brain problem and full acknowledgment that as of this date no person has proven that the mind is dependent on the brain, let's for the moment accept that the mind of the individual is somehow initiated by the brain. Regarding electromagnetism and its relationship to matter, you are probably aware that our planet acts as a giant electromagnet, which is why we have our north and south poles. Our experience of living, consisting of both physical reality and the delusional reality of mind, is encased in the electromagnetism of this planet. Our common reality has been consistently influenced by our planet since the dawn of our existence as a species. Since we can't avoid the effects of our planet, we can't escape the influence of electromagnetism on our brain. One might ultra-think that the progression of our physical reality and delusional reality would be limited due to the localized influence of electromagnetism driven by the earth.

As observers with long-range measuring devices, we earth-lings seek to see and influence faraway matter. These measurements are limited by our technology, mental capability, and physical senses. For instance, a three-year-old child may see our moon, but not being able to deductively comprehend what he or she is truly seeing, the moon is then an insignificant piece of the child's delusional reality.

Through our science we explore further into the depths of the universe each day. With this action we stretch our observations, giving our reality a chance to expand. Still, unless the information is comprehended by our mind, neither our physical nor our delusional reality actually expands. When or if we observe an unknown 'something' from afar, would our reality about aliens expand without a lucid understanding of what we see? If I truly see an alien and comprehend the subject as a rock, would that extraterrestrial being actually exist or not? The answer is no, it doesn't exist. I have observed yet another rock, not an alien. My impressions of reality create my very reality. This is all that matters to me specifically.

Some researchers believe that at its root, the universe itself is nothing but information and data simply waiting to be understood. Could it be that each and every time we comprehend fresh data our scrutiny simultaneously expands the presence of physical reality itself? Given that our comprehension is limited by our own delusion and that delusion is created under the effects of forces related to our earth, could it be that we must move well beyond the earth to expand reality to its full potential?

CHAPTER 6

GAMMA RAYS ARE COSMIC ERASERS

Some of the more fascinating questions of science and metaphysics deal with issues like whether we ever prove there is other intelligent life in the cosmos. Let's consider the issue, but first I want to frame the topic within the context of my own mind-myth. My ultra-thinking has already led me to create three Ultrathoughts:

1. Life exists beyond our planet, and some of this life can be considered intelligent.
2. Technology gets better over time until and unless something major happens to change the paradigm.
3. Intelligent life besides *H. sapiens* seeks to comprehend the cosmos.

Given my mind-myth view of truth, the more poignant question is not "Does intelligent life exist?" but "Where are they?"

Doesn't it stand to reason that some other life-form, whether biologically living or artificially constructed, would not only have access to their own sophisticated technology but would have done something to make themselves known? Furthermore, given how far we *H. Sapiens* have advanced in our brief 250 thousand to 300 thousand years, if their bizarre technology is a billion or even a million years more advanced than ours, sensibly we would have seen some trace of that technology.

In consideration of this topic, several notable individuals conclude that the most reasonable answer to these types of questions is that we experience our lives in a simulation. Advocates of the idea take for granted, as do I, that at least one if not many more intelligent beings would be so far advanced as to have produced sophisticated models that go far beyond our wildest comprehension. It is surmised that these models or simulations are capable of producing such texture and richness that participants become so engaged as to lose a sense of themselves. But here's where the advocates lose me. They believe we are currently participating in the aliens' big computer game and are simply unaware of our state of existence. In my view, that goes too far.

My personal Ultrathoughts lead me in a different direction regarding "where are they" questions. But let me first admit that this simulation idea, while extremely unlikely, is not entirely without mathematical support. If we strictly consider the math, and that's the key to supporting the premise—math—this idea that we only exist in a simulation is among the best of any number of highly improbable possibilities. Of course, to say "highly improbable" is to gloss over the math itself. The statistical likelihood that we have no physical presence in a reality and the entire species exists in a simulation is so remote that it's just barely more plausible than the math necessary to support a belief that we live in a multiverse. The practical statistics in support of any of these theories are nearly as likely as the next. Whether the odds that the simulation idea is correct are a billion to one or a trillion to one doesn't matter; nothing will ever be proven. In short, no human will ever know the nature of reality or the cosmos, so think what you will. Your wild guess is basically as good as that of any PhD on the planet.

I seek a better understanding of reality and our underlying purpose. Though I've determined "no answer" is the most likely answer, I still search for answers because this is simply what a left-brainer does. I remind myself that I'm living a delusion, so I can undertake this search without getting overly-obsessed or discouraged by the journey. It simply makes sense to me that given the vastness of the cosmos *something* should be "out there." Unlike a scientist who lives a delusion yet can't admit it for fear of betraying a dogma of belief, I admit my lot.

I take it for granted that beyond our planet there exist other intelligent life forms. Some of these are made of organic molecules, others not. It is certainly plausible that on distant planets organic life could be locked inside soil, rock, molten material, or oceans of ice; regardless, these beings could be so bizarre that we may not at first even recognize them as life. As a set of organic molecules, the creatures may look like a stegosaurus, a sponge, an amoeba, an inexplicable type of virus, or your brother-in-law. Regarding artificial life, the potential variations are virtually limitless. Just try to imagine something like a translucent sheet of nanobots exploring the galaxy for a billion years! My ultra-thinking assumes that several if not millions of forms of life exist in physical presence beyond our planet, some organically based others not. Potentially some of these are billions of years older than our species. So then, back to a great question: Where are they?

The answer could lie in how God assures the primacy of organic life in the cosmos. Let's consider supernova events and gamma rays in general as akin to tools used by the Godhead. Supernova explosions, the explosions of stars, impact planets and even entire galaxies millions of light years away via bursts of energy. When a star explodes, if it's big enough to fall within the category of a supernova event, it disperses nearly incalculable amounts of energy, which is expelled in the form of gamma radiation. Cosmologists tell us this energy burst acts as a kind of cosmic eraser. Gamma rays produced in a supernova event form something like a shock wave, or tsunami, of energy disrupting other energy fields which up to that point had been stable. That stable energy is often expressed as a magnetic field, as is the case with our planet. Earth naturally produces a stable curtain of this magnetic energy, which acts like a protective umbrella shielding us from killer radiation. Similar planets to ours probably do similar things and protect their life within a sphere of influence. Energy curtains of protection are inherently created by everything from magnets to entire solar systems. Cosmologists surmise that disruption caused by a supernova event and its gamma ray tsunami is so complete that this protective curtain can be literally ripped away. Entire planets and solar systems can lose their protection, leaving all life, organic or artificial, exposed and vulnerable for eons. If such an event impacted our planet today, it would soon wipe out all artificial life and possibly all electronic equipment. In a relatively short period of time we would find all machines, software programs, and magnetized data to be rendered useless with little or no hope of recovery. This may be why we don't encounter extraterrestrial, artificially-based life. Supernova events are erasers of artificial life and disrupters of organic life.

Organic life is fundamentally less susceptible to the effect of gamma bursts than artificial life. Don't misunderstand: a supernova anywhere near earth would absolutely kill *most* organic life within minutes or days, either because of the gamma rays or the resulting atmospheric changes impacting physical weather patterns. We can assume most every form of organic life bigger than a pebble would ultimately become extinct. Some organic life, particularly that locked deep in the soil, would survive and could (due to lack of competition for resources) thrive underground for millennia. While blasts of gamma radiation are not necessarily good for our biology, they are not always fatal.

DNA, a unique collection of molecules forming the code of biological life, has been observed to use radiation to create new variations, which we call mutations. Possibly this phenomenon,

DNA transforming while artificial life dies, further indicates that primacy has been given to biological life. All matter of the universe, dead or living, at some time will be subject to the influence of gamma rays. Organic life has an advantage that is built into the cosmos. This advantage leads me to conclude that living organisms will outlast any artificially based life-form.

We have already found an example of the likely product of a gamma burst right next door. This may one day provide support of my Ultrathought. Scientists are fairly confident that at one time Mars had an atmosphere. That atmosphere, it is theorized, was blown away eons ago, possibly by the gamma rays of a supernova. Scientists had assumed Mars was a bundle of dead matter incapable of supporting the organic compounds of life. The lack of any atmospheric protection from the energy of radiation led scientists to assume there has never been any life on Mars. Recently, however, these same scientists have begun to change their minds on the heels of more sophisticated experiments. It is increasingly likely that very soon we'll have objective proof that Mars does have organic compounds and the planet may either have had or does still harbor life. The evidence may have always been present, existing merely a couple of meters below the surface.

Confirmation of life on Mars may one day drive home my Ultrathought: gamma bursts cleanse the universe of artificial life, and that assures an advantage to organic life. Advanced societies have existed and still do with technology far more sophisticated than our own. Their robot explorers do from time to time stretch far from their home. But their technology, like our own, is limited in its advancement by design of the Godhead. Any artificial technology can only advance so far before God wipes the slate clean through a gamma burst of pure energy. Supernovas serve as cosmic erasers and thereby allow organic life to prosper and remain superior over dead matter.

CHAPTER 7

TIME, A LIMITING PERCEPTION

At the risk of discussing the single most over-analyzed topic of physics, let's contemplate time. We understand that time is relative, but what does that actually mean? Plainly speaking, time can be considered a property constantly influenced by its surroundings. Time expresses a presence dependent on the context of its surrounding speed of motion and acceleration. Our time as experienced on earth while standing at sea level is a given constant of x. Everyone in your proximity shares this constant. They all share the same time. Nevertheless, if your partner was flying above in a rocket traveling at any speed, your partner's time is not x, but some slight variation of x. The reason is that your partner's speed and acceleration are different than yours standing still at sea level. The time of your observed partner never actually changes from his or her perspective, but relative to your own it does. Hence, any and all expressions of time are "relative" statements of fact within a given domain of applicability. There is no such thing as universal time.

Relativity is an interpretation made by the observer. Therefore, while time is relative, time appears constant in our daily experience. It is effectively "background noise" without a comparative observation. We don't often consider any time other than our own, and certainly don't really care what time it may be on the Voyager 1 spacecraft launched in 1977 moving at a speed of 38,610 miles per hour. By the way, physicists believe the time on the spacecraft would be maybe a few seconds ahead of our own. Given the number of variables, precise calculations of time on the craft are elusive. There is, unequivocally, no precise way to measure the difference between two clocks that are not physically located together. Any measurement of time is both contextual and subjective. With that said, by the time Voyager 1 reaches its destination in another forty thousand years, the spacecraft should be one and a half to two hours ahead of Earth time. The craft will arrive before, in our view, it does! That is challenging to comprehend, but the statement is accurate.

Why would we have difficulty comprehending the nature of time? Because we are immersed in our shared understanding of the idea. Every person or animal with whom we interact with assumes time is important. It is, therefore relevant to their existence. Our society agrees time is real and isn't particularly concerned with philosophical discussions about time and meta ideas. As a result, people don't stop and ponder the nature of time. We use time and agree time exists despite the fact that it cannot be proven a manifest truth. In order to effectively use time, we've developed a related idea.

Time, within our mind, is perceived as progressing or moving in a linear fashion. Time can't be linear, because time itself is but an idea. There are no such things as the "past" and "future" in a strict sense. Time is not a physical thing, so how can a physical body move through a concept (time) void of all matter? Maybe we haven't met any people or robots from the future because the future doesn't and will never actually exist. With that specific Ultrathought off my chest, time is a useful and necessary concept, particularly when an observer seeks to consider motion.

I consider time in this section, not to rehash Einstein, but gain a better understanding of both mind and the importance of perspective in creating a reality. Once we recognize that time is nothing but an idea absent a relative comparison, we can understand the importance of the observer in any measurement. Remove the observer and there is no measurement, no time. The observer is therefore key.

Still, time as an idea does seem to exist in a sense even without an observer. Like Plato's idea of the apple being something separate from the physical fruit, we can retain an idea of time without the measurement. So, if time is a meta thing, and measurement is optional this may explain why, when absorbed in a task, I don't consciously conceive of movement or the passing of time. Time seems to "slip away" without my creating an awareness of its passing regardless of my cognizance of the event. On the other hand, time drags on endlessly when watching a clock or creating a heightened awareness of its passage. Time seems to have a kind of dual nature. In my intellect I can choose to recognize it or not, yet my biology seems to create time automatically. My biology is an observer of time despite my intellect.

As previously discussed, every atom shivers or vibrates for unknown reasons. This Brownian motion is fundamental to physical matter, meaning motion itself is fundamental to the universe. This motion facilitates a measuring of the passage of the number of historical shivers. I surmise that any form of complex life seeking to measure the wasting of its physical existence does measure time whether that measurement occurs in the intellect or the subconscious. A primary reason animal life should care about time is because physical existence as an organized collection of molecules is subject to a wasting away of energy expelled through motion. To perceive of the wasting, the organism would require a measurement of the motion. The observer subconsciously compares "before and after" states, creating a relative measurement. My subconscious mind, my very biology, wants to track the age of the physical body since the organism deems the measurement useful.

Our use of time evolves as we do. When we choose to focus on the passage of time within our conscious awareness, we notice the benefits of measurement. Our construct of time aids in planning, organizing, and strategizing. The advantage is magnified when we share a common perception of time and measure its passing with mutually agreed accuracy. As societies evolved we became more focused on time, and eventually most of humanity failed to appreciate that time itself is a byproduct of our need to preform consistent relative comparisons. Time is relative, but the observer is the facilitator of that relativity.

The body created time, and the conscious mind created the complex time we take for granted today. As our species evolved I suspect we happened to notice a very useful aspect of the measurement of time. Measurement relies upon a point of perspective. In math, we know the reference point as zero. With regard to the measurement of time within a conscious intellect, that point is the present. Having the present as a reference point, the mind can write a narrative that lucidly describes the past and the future in reference to the present. Eventually, the mind came to use time as a tool in its creation of mind-myth. This use of time allowed humans to organize ideas efficiently in a linear manner. Such a linear progression of ideas is the very definition of a story. We all know we remember better when we pin an event to a story, and this is exactly why intelligent humans need time; its creation allows us to maintain a dense narrative.

In short, time is not a physical thing. Time doesn't exist in an absolute sense and certainly can't be linear. Time as a meta concept exists for various reasons: to subconsciously track our lifespan, to live productively in an organized society, and to organize our memories in a manner the brain can access. Furthermore, as a meta creation time is perceived as passing in a linear fashion.

The linear assumption about time makes it challenging to conceptualize topics like quantum entanglement, relative time, and the superposition of all possible states. Without changing our fundamental perception of time, most of us can't grasp what "instantaneous" actually means. We view all events in a linear context of past, present, and future.

I suggest we train our minds to recognize that time is wholly optional. We shouldn't deny the worthiness of time, but to ultra-think we need to move beyond our indoctrinated view of time and recognize what it actually is and is not. To become enlightened, one must be able to step away from the limits of their existing mental narrative. We respect the mind but elect to be more than mind on auto-pilot. No past, present, or future is a manifest reality. Each are simply perceptions viewed within a context of a linear time assumption. Even the words "before" and "after" become irrelevant, absent time. This leads me to wonder whether I should re-ultra-think my position on the afterlife and soul of humans. If there is no "after" would there be an "afterlife"?

I haven't had the emotional energy to revisit the Godhead in the context of my most recent notions about time. In the "future" I hope to spend more "time" on this concept of self being fundamentally unbound to the physical realm. If I do, I'll update the *www.ultrathoughts.com* website. After all the website could probably interact with a timeless version of you easier anyway. Then again, maybe I've already wasted too much time on this subject.

CHAPTER 8

HOMO SAPIENS 2.0

I t has become fashionable of late to consider the next version of humanity. Whether our next stage comes as a result of the natural forces of evolution, the direct hand of God, or the dynamic relationship between people and machines, more of us are convinced *Homo sapiens* version *2.0* is on the horizon. This view is certainly not new. Still, today this long-time theme of various religions is gaining acceptance among an elite class of scientists. What was once considered the irrational visions of religious nuts or entertaining sci-fi is being seriously studied by our best and brightest.

The idea of a new and improved model of our biological species is certainly a worthy topic for ultra-thinking because it leads to a deeper understanding of ourselves and the dynamics of our existence. In order for our species to branch off and become *H. sapiens 2.0*, our distant child would need to be significantly different than ourselves. An understanding of the nature of those differences requires that we first appreciate why we are dissimilar from our own ancestors. Such an evaluation is far more difficult than it sounds.

We merely have traces of our early cousins; bone, etchings, and tools. Scientists, in a few cases have had success in mapping DNA segments from ancient tissue. Of course, DNA is of limited value in understanding the true nature of the creature, and while artifacts may provide hints, they are far from definitive evidence of anything. By combining all available information, anthropologists believe they have some understanding of how our ancestors looked, hunted, walked, and lived. Stretching their theories further some are confident they even know a bit about how these people thought. Did they have spiritual awareness? Some researchers review various artifacts and are quite confident they know, others disagree. In my view, it's quite a stretch to assume we actually know how pre-modern peoples like Neanderthal or Flores man thought when we aren't even sure that the evidence we find is actually from the people we are theorizing about.

In considering the future of our species, significant research is focused on the merger of human and technology. Though the specifics vary, most believe it rather obvious that people and machine will effectively merge and be "better" as a result. Today's augmented reality games and bioimplant usage point to a not-so-distant future, merely decades from now, when our species is enhanced beyond our comprehension. We will still be this same species but the species will have incredible abilities aided by robotics, nanotechnology and mental augmentation. Of course, these scientific advancements will be accomplished with the use of machine or artificial intelligence (AI).

I suggest that AI may be the key in urging the evolution of our new model. Our quest for an easy and enjoyable life may prove to be our Achilles heel. A physical being that is not challenged or exercised wastes away. In an ironic twist, though through augmentation we would appear to have incredible capabilities amplified through AI, we would actually be far less "special" than we have ever been. We would have become machine dependent.

Left unchecked, there is little doubt artificial intelligence will eventually facilitate changes to our animal. Evolution from our very limited understanding of the process seems to take a bit of time. Therefore without DNA modification technologies to expedite the progression our specific species may exist with AI facilitated augmentation for hundreds if not thousands of years, although eventually, the dawn of a new species would appear.

Be reminded that the evolution of one species to another involves far more than physical characteristics. In ways we don't understand your physiology is intertwined with the non-physical essence of your person. The essence of you is closely tied to your mind. You become the person you think you are. A new species of hominins could simply express different action and thought than predecessors, thereby qualifying as *H. sapiens 2.0* although the physical features of each are identical.

My ultra-thinking determines that for a relatively brief period of time our specific human species will remain dominant on the planet. Having a body which is enabled through highly engineered augmentation we can't yet comprehend how this will change the mind. Reminding you there is evidence that patterns of thought do seem to be inheritable traits, I believe our offspring will one day be born having a different mental orientation.

I surmise that eventually the very tenor and theme of a mind-myth narrative created by a segment of our species which has evolved to optimize augmentation will be different than that of others. Just imagine living your life having the library of congress, or a global road map simply there in your *head*. As more societies seek the advantages of an augmented citizenry, this innate way of thinking will become the preferred way of thought. Within roughly five generations of its immergence this "different" way of thinking will come to dominate the species. What would life be like for a person who has an internet search engine seamlessly integrated within their mind? That is just one example of what is in store for our children of the future.

Though a mentally augmented person would think significantly different than we do, I suppose they would still seek affirmation. Today we commonly derive much of our affirmation via an innate sense of spirituality; however, we aren't shy about obtaining comfort from material substance either. The augmented person will constantly be empowered and emboldened through AI enhancement. In the future a highly-augmented human being may build a myth that relies so much on the material that it neglects the spiritual entirely. A mind-myth immersed exclusively within the physical realm aided by AI will unintentionally, yet continually deny the worthiness of the spiritual realm. I ultra-think that as humanity continues to augment vast numbers of people at a very early age, we will cause our species to morph. This new class of beings would have absolutely no spiritual awareness because they simply didn't need any. Thinking meaningfully different than *H. sapiens* this creature would qualify as an entirely new species. *H. sapiens 2.0* will ultimately appear because of a change in thought pattern not as a result of any significant physical change.

Our species, *H. sapiens* prime, may coexist with version *2.0* for eons just as Neanderthal coexisted with *H. sapiens*. Eventually, however, *2.0* will dominate the planet and largely overwhelm prime. *2.0* may even push its presence beyond the solar system ruling its range as a type of demigod hominin unless, of course, my Ultrathought regarding cosmic erasers proves prophetic. As previously stated, it is entirely possible that all machine intelligence is simply erased from the solar system. With that qualifier disclosed, I suggest that one day members of prime may see that *H. sapiens 2.0* isn't the last of our lineage.

It's commonly accepted by futurists that, eventually, AI will have no need for biological hominins. Artificial General Intelligence (AGI) machines are on the horizon. These truly autonomous machines will have the ability to learn any intellectual task and will be common place on the planet within 1,000 to 10,000 years. Regardless of the timeframe, this form of 'life' will be so far advanced of both AI and version *2.0* that machines, not hominins, will eventually dominate all that is physical in the galaxy. But, before that occurs *H. sapiens 3.0* will evolve from human version *2.0*.

Version *3.0* of the more distant future will not bother to learn anything organically because all knowledge can literally be gleaned through technology. Having little sense of wonder this creature will have a dull mind-myth when compared to *2.0* and certainly *H. sapiens* prime. Version *3.0* may express what appears to be casual brilliance but without nurturing any depth of mind, the human will be utterly ignorant when 'offline.' Having no mental depth, this last evolution of 'us' will probably be a fool of very limited mental or physical capacity due to its near-total reliance on technology.

I ultra-think that it is highly probable that *H. sapiens 3.0* will be the very last species from our line of modern humans. Will a somewhat intelligent chimpanzee still exist in the wild 100,000 years from now? Probably. Will a curiously intelligent cuttlefish exist in the sea? Most certainly. Will any human-like ape version, *H. sapiens* prime, *2.0* or even version *3.0* exist anywhere 100 millennia from now? I suggest that if one does it may only be a curiosity of the AGI constructed zoo.

We are the only animal on the planet today that has the innate ability to contemplate the Godhead. We reflexively express this tendency as children and the inclination continues through adulthood provided that we attempt to show deference. Like an innate need for love, companionship, or affirmation, we need to seek the Godhead to be fulfilled. Certainly, we can train ourselves to deny a need for love, and we can do the same with respect to the spiritual realm. That training can be overt, or it can simply come as a result of preoccupation with other matters, regardless it is an anathema to the species.

Documented trends show that in Western society our brethren are neglecting Godhead predisposition. Therefore, it is possible a new version of our species will arrive far sooner than many believe. Today thousands if not millions are maturing to create a reality bubble that is lethargic mentally and neglectful of what makes them special on this planet. I meet a number of people who project outright hatred toward all that is spiritual. While this is a bit annoying, it's better than what others seem to be doing. More and more people deny the very idea of the meta. To resent or hate the spiritual realm one must have at least contemplated its very existence, but to deny any possibility of the Godhead within the mind is to be a rather common animal.

Whether it's the result of individual choice, the natural forces of evolution, the direct hand of God, or the dynamic relationship between us and AI, is unimportant. To be a-spiritual urges our annihilation. We have but one truly unique characteristic: the ability to contemplate deeply. Such contemplation seems to include if not focus on the Godhead. To suppress or neglect this feature is to deny our very humanity.

Before leaving this discussion I want to give you a thought to ultra-think. Is it possible that we are the dullest incarnation of the family to date? Is it conceivable that whatever species predated us in our family line, this predecessor *was* the better version of us? In such case, we are not prime but version *H. sapiens 1.0*. I'm starting to wonder if there is an underlying reason for the double helix structure of DNA. You know the image. The twisted spiral pattern. Could it be that we are just another step on a downward spiral staircase to becoming a common animal?

CHAPTER 9

ADVANCED TECHNOLOGY AND ANCIENT CIVILIZATION

People who are overly logical, people who are strongly oriented toward the left hemisphere, need answers and we get unusually frustrated when we can't find them. Of course, answers don't exist for every question. Still, certain challenges, problems that are clearly of the physical realm, should present solvable problems. Given ten, one hundred, or one thousand years, someone somewhere should be able explain something as basic as how a heavy stone is moved across the desert for hundreds of miles. Yet for some reason our society full of scientists aided by super-computers can't seem to figure certain things out. Since the PhD's either can't or won't answer our questions, we shall have no shame in coming up with our own ideas, our own Ultrathoughts about the ancients.

My own questions regarding the ancients often revolve around megalithic structures. More specifically:

- Is it plausible to assume that only very crude technology was used to create these edifices, and if so, can we adequately replicate the specific methods used?
- Is it plausible that humanity had at its disposal some type of advanced or yet unknown technology that aided in the construction of these structures?
- Is it plausible that *H. sapiens* was not involved in the creation of the truly megalithic structures we see today?

In case you're not familiar with the phrase, megalithic structures, these are systematically arranged collections of huge stones, buildings or monuments constructed using natural or modified stones weighing tens, hundreds, and occasionally, over one thousand tons. In many cases we aren't sure how old the structures are, therefore these sites may not be strictly prehistoric. I'm referring to locations like Stonehenge (England), Easter Island (central Pacific), the Giza Plateau (Egypt), Machu Picchu (Peru), Osaka Castle (Japan), Yangshan (China), and Baalbek (Lebanon).

For simplicity, let's first consider one specific monolith—the statue of Ramesses II of Thebes, Egypt. Today this statue is found in ruins, but estimates of its incredibly hard pink granite construction put its weight in the range of one thousand tons, having a seated height of over thirty-five feet. The supposed quarry from which the granite came is located 170 miles away. Its age of origin is uncertain, but there are indications it first appeared on or about the reign of Ramesses II, circa 1250 BCE, nearly 3,300 years ago. In support of mainstream views Egyptologists tell us that although they can't prove it, it is safe to assume these "primitives" dragged this one-thousand-ton piece of stone across the desert using simple ropes and then placed it on a barge for further transport. Using similar methods, we couldn't do this with manpower today—even if we attempt to do so with our superior ropes and pullies. As far as placing a block this size on a barge; well, they have no idea how that could be accomplished. Since we don't encounter object weights like this often, let me remind you that one thousand tons is about the weight of thirteen space shuttles or Boeing 737 airliners, each weighing roughly seventy-five tons. You understood that correctly. This one statue weighed the same as thirteen commercial jets!

This statue has challenged archeologists for hundreds of years. It is presented as fact that the ancients moved this massive block and then worked it exclusively through the use of copper chisels, cold and hot water to cause cracking, and pounding stones and sand for final polish. My ultra-thinking tells me the advocates of at least some of these theories are either the dumbest group of scientists on the planet, or I'm being lied too.

One would think moving or creating something like this would be worthy of a diagram or plaque, yet we find no explanation. Some researchers, those less dogmatic in their approach to mysteries, remind us there is no way to even be positive the statue was always a carving of Ramesses II. Egyptians often repurposed art and monuments. It is possible the Ramesses II we find today could be a rework of a far earlier monument.

Of course, no discussion of ancient technology and science can neglect the Great Pyramid of Giza. This pyramid and its surrounding complex appear to be a precision observatory built to technical standards that would be difficult to replicate today. Our experts again have theories but ultimately can merely speculate as to how this feat of construction was accomplished to such a precise technical standard. The specifics of this particular site are so far ahead of what we perceive as the capabilities of the Egyptians that even a few career archeologists conclude the dynastic Egyptians themselves may not have built and certainly couldn't have designed the Great Pyramid given the "facts" at hand.

Though the mainstream won't speculate beyond an admission that there is more to know, certain alternative researchers conclude that the dynastic Egyptians simply co-opted much of what we see today, including fundamental aspects of the Giza Plateau. They theorize that later Egyptian peoples maintained, adapted, and built additional structures during the dynastic period of Egypt. Alternative theorists suggest that while it is remotely possible they may have re-built much of the Great Pyramid, there is absolutely no way that dynastic Egyptians themselves had the knowledge necessary to design and originate the entire plan for the Giza Plateau.

It is an absolute fact that the dynastic Egyptians built certain monuments of Thebes and pyramids across their empire. That much is not in dispute. But it is certainly possible that they themselves didn't possess the ability to create all of the truly stunning structures for which we give them credit. Some would go so far as to say the first builders of numerous megalithic and sophisticated structures like the Great Pyramid were a different and distinct society of *H. sapiens* all together. They surmise that this far more ancient society of people had different information that has since been "lost."

In defense of more traditional views, we must admit that building a pyramid structure itself is not difficult. However, specifically considering the Great Pyramid, its complexity of design and construction is another matter. A valid comparison between other pyramids and the Great Pyramid would be equivalent to comparing the design and construction of an average home to a forty-story high-rise. Obviously, two entirely different levels of skill are required.

We are told by traditional Egyptologists that all the structures of ancient Egypt were built without much more than manual labor, copper axes, and string. Recall that during the earliest period of dynastic Egypt, that of the supposed construction of the Great Pyramid, this society didn't have the wheel, bronze, or iron. Naturally we assume they fully understood algebra, but we've found no proof of any advanced mathematics being used until hundreds of years after the supposed construction date of the Great Pyramid.

Regarding their technology, we are informed that somehow the Egyptians, prior to 3200 BCE, managed to make precision cuts on hard stones such as granite, quartz, granodiorite, syenite, and basalt. Today we use hydraulic powered diamond bit technology to cut these stones. The stones can't efficiently be cut with softer metals, like copper, yet we clearly observe cut marks and core-drilling. This is strong evidence of machine work.

The mainstream tells us the supposed machines of ancient Egypt were nothing more than manual labor aided by drills using stick and string. The drill bit was either made or enhanced by copper and a slurry mixture of ground quartz. Frankly, this insults our intelligence. Anyone can clearly see interior corners squared to laser-like precision on pink granite, the rounded of bowls made from diorite or rock crystal, and hollow cores reaching several inches. While sand and water will facilitate the cutting of hard stone given enough time, and it is true that hard stone river rock becomes as round as any ball given years of abrasion, the method can't, under any circumstance, account for the cutting of certain angles, interior corners, blade marks, and scoop markings on hard stone. A simple observation confirms the ancients had something more than rudimentary technology.

The evidence for my Ultrathoughts on ancient technology is ipso facto; the megalithic structures exist, the machine marks are present, and there is no reasonable way to reproduce them using primitive technological methods. These structures were built using some sort of advanced technology—a technology that not only rivaled but may have exceeded our own capabilities. If scientific evidence of my conclusions exists, the public at large is not privy. If some scholars are aware of objective proof of my conjecture, they choose to keep it concealed.

Be reminded that your mind slants the phrase "advanced technology." What I am referring to is not necessarily some type of crazy laser or nuclear-powered drill bit. Advanced technology could possibly wield sound produced using benign-looking instruments to manipulate sound waves. It could even be unique mixtures of chemicals in advanced recipes that soften stone or create incredible mixtures of concrete. Furthermore, don't rule out the possibility of the truly outrageous. Conceivably they had a keen understanding of our cosmos and used inexplicable capabilities of mind or naturally occurring magnetism to manipulate gravity.

Mainstream archeologists insist that no society before the Romans, circa 300 BCE, used a high-quality concrete recipe and that it is silly to speculate about things like stone softening or levitation. Nevertheless, many of us insist there are absolutely prima facie examples of quality concrete and stone softening that exist across many parts of the globe. One doesn't need to view these sites in person to plainly see the obvious in photographs. The mainstream view simply doesn't make sense, and even my own "wild ideas" are better than lies perpetuated in defense of scientific dogma.

Countless examples of stonework exist in Egypt that lend credence to the inkling that either concrete or stone softening was used but the single best example of concrete or softening is 7,500 miles away in Machu Picchu Peru. If you are not familiar with the site Google it briefly. Mainstream archeology tells us the walls of Machu Picchu were made by the Inca people using traditional methods of masonry, which again means the use of copper chisels and pounding stones. They tell us the work occurred merely 500–700 years ago even though no one today can replicate the technique. Our scholars tell us that the Inca had unlimited manpower; therefore, although we can't replicate their stonework, we should trust the opinion of mainstream archeologists—the Inca built Machu Picchu. Be reminded that, unlike the Egyptians, the Inca had no written language and did not leave any sort of documentation regarding construction. If we assume the Inca actually did create what we see today, there are only two plausible answers in explanation of how they did it: high-quality concrete or stone softening.

How can we accurately even date a stone or an entire archeological site if a later culture usurps another and fully integrates its structures within their own society? What the archeologists often do is fail to remind us that their dating of sites relies on carbon dating of organic material found near or underneath stones that are presumed to have been stationary until sampled. There is no consistently accurate way to date stone, so they're left with attempting to date the surrounding area. Using this method, they can never consider the whole story, the possibility that a later society simply obliterated the record of its predecessor.

As is the case with the dynastic Egyptians, it is very likely that the Inca culture of Peru improved or modified numerous sites they didn't originally build. What we find across South America, including Machu Picchu, are sites that were occupied by the Inca from roughly 1100–1550 CE. Occupation doesn't necessarily mean construction. Therefore, we can never rule out the idea that at least some of these sites predate the Inca by thousands of years.

When we ultra-think how ancient cultures could have cut hardened stone or moved blocks weighing a thousand tons, it makes sense that we should shed the dogma of mainstream archeology. We're told that we currently possess the most advanced and sophisticated technology ever developed in the solar system. Scientists inform us that technology progresses in a linear fashion. We are the best and most productive examples of our species. Allowing mainstream ideological bias to box in our thoughts leaves us with ludicrous answers to questions concerning ancient technology.

In contrast to the mainstream I suggest that some sort of advanced technology existed many millennia ago that facilitated the creation of megalithic structures, period. It is no affront to the world to admit this, therefore, I'm left to ponder why a rather benign fact is being denied by the establishment. To seriously contemplate the question of why experts, paid and supported by various governments would hide historical or scientific truth from the public, we should attempt to understand the interplay between technology, society, and even politics. What is the impact of reintroducing or bringing forth a truly advanced technology?

Technological advancement always displaces some workers. Of course, today our operating assumption is that new technology creates as many job opportunities as it destroys. In truth, this is a provable myth—a line provided by ardent capitalists and big business. Technological advances displace workers and destroy communities. In time, advances may eventually bring forth new opportunities for workers but certainly this isn't guaranteed to happen. This is not a political statement or rant against progress; it is common sense. Progress is good, but machines replace beasts. Politicians and governments are left to manage the transition.

A question I keep coming back to is: what if the ancients had a recipe for high-quality concrete, and we rediscovered that same technique? To contemplate this question, I've found it helpful to first consider societal dynamics at the time the mysteries of Egypt were being systematically explored by archeologists in the modern age (circa 1800 CE).

France was the principal source of not only funding but enthusiasm for this period in history. It's important to remember that France had recently come through decades of civil strife culminating in the French Revolution during the 1790s. France had also recently pushed the English out of Egypt. As the fighting ceased, French explorers led the charge into Egypt. The French sought to claim Egypt and in doing so they "rediscovered" what was in plain sight for thousands of years. Of course, the details surrounding the sites were long gone, but the structures were substantially intact and their construction needed to be investigated. It was left to the French to inform us of Egyptian history. In doing so they formed the foundations for our beliefs about ancient technology.

In this era, European stone masons commanded a huge amount of political clout. Stone craft was a big business not unlike truck driving in the 1960s or banking in the 2000s. The industry employed thousands of hard working and rather volatile people who had lived through decades of conflict. These tradesmen had a steady source of income, working stone, which was incredibly important for French society and they kept political leaders on their toes for fear of yet another revolution.

Here's my ultra-thinking. If the early French explorers of ancient Egypt, financed and controlled as an adjunct to the military, had rediscovered an advanced concrete recipe they may not have been allowed to share this discovery. This single invention would disrupt their society. The reintroduction of some type of miraculous laborsaving concrete or stone softening technique would put thousands of stone masons out of work. Since the government of France was funding the exploration of ancient Egypt, doesn't it fit that had they become aware of such a recipe they would have preferred the information not be disseminated?

Naturally, this type of conspiracy ultra-thinking is pure conjecture. However, we do know governments and power brokers keep information from the public for various reasons. With regard to the empire of Napoleon specifically, we know for a fact that this conqueror had a history of disparaging the culture of a defeated nation. In 1797, French troops destroyed manuscripts of composers and musicians of Venice (*see,* the story of the all-female music ensemble of the Ospedale della Pieta) for the simple reason of protecting French national pride.

As I consider the politics of the 1800s, I see a very rational reason for keeping a recipe for concrete or something similar a secret. You may think any such action would be rather silly, but I don't. Reasons are always subject to the facts and circumstances of the day. I believe there are often times when information should be concealed from the masses.

Without a doubt, the ancients had some types of technology unknown to the majority of people alive today. Who among us knows what, at this very instant, I won't speculate. Nevertheless, I will speculate that there is more to this story. I, among others, believe later cultures inherited the truly megalithic structures we observe today. Meaning the dynastic Egyptians never had to drag a thousand-ton block through the desert, and the Incas themselves didn't need to shape the walls of Machu Picchu. I suggest the megalithic structures we study today, most of them anyway, were already in place and these later societies merely adapted them for their own purposes. It is also plausible to assume that actual technological information was provided to these later peoples from their predecessors, but such information was sacred knowledge never to be disseminated amongst the commoners.

Finally, I suggest it is worth considering from a fair and open mind, the idea that our species, *H. sapiens*, didn't create every single ancient site we come across. Though I won't categorically reject the idea, I'm not suggesting that extraterrestrials created megalithic structures. I am merely reminding the reader that other species of hominins resided on this planet for far more years than we can even imagine. It should not be ruled out that an unknown technology— like a method to create high-quality concrete, soften stone, or even dare I say, levitate stone—was mastered by an ancient even yet undiscovered variety of hominins. Admittedly, this is highly speculative; however, these ideas are no more implausible than the ridiculous idea that soft metal can cut granite with precision, or that 1000-ton blocks were lifted and dragged miles using nothing more than crude robes and manpower.

The ancient technology question is fun and captivates the mind of ultra-thinkers, yet it pales in comparison to the more significant question: How old is human civilization?

As the story has gone for more than two hundred years, mainstream science has informed us that the Mesopotamian civilization of Sumer, circa 3500 BCE more or less, was the first to develop writing and agriculture. The island of Malta housed a civilization that archeology dates to about the same period, but others believe it to go back at least one millennium if not two earlier. The dynastic Egyptians made their presence felt about 3100 BCE, and the Minoans, 2600 BCE. Asia and India were home to somewhat advanced civilizations. Unfortunately, due to the dynamics and density of the current population in these areas today, we don't have significant evidence that points to dates much earlier than 1600 BCE, apart from the Indus Valley culture. Little verifiable evidence exists, but the dating of limited artifacts indicates the beginnings of this Indus Valley society goes back as far as 3000 BCE. We're informed that prior to these civilizations any society built by our species was so inconsequential that it barely deserved to be recognized as civilization.

With due deference to the majority of mainstream archeologists and their anthropologist cohorts, I must discuss Göbekli Tepe. This unusual archeological site located in southeastern Turkey single-handedly undermines the preceding paragraph. A consensus is forming that this site can be documented as having existed ten thousand to thirteen thousand years ago. Though the artifacts aren't technically megalithic and may not even hint at forms of advanced stone work, the nature of the site certainly documents members of a rather complex society walked these hills located in Eurasia circa 8000 to 11000 BCE! The evidence lies in contrast to the scholarly opinion of anthropologists who insist that no hominin species had a sophisticated society until well after the time of the supposed Mesopotamian invention of agriculture. Dating of this one site proves our ancestors could not have been purely hunter-gatherers until a few thousand years ago. The accepted theory on the evolution of human civilization is bogus.

Sumer, our supposed oldest site, is roughly half the age of Göbekli Tepe. I urge you to pause and give that a bit of thought - HALF the age. Mainstream archeologists inform us that the so-called cradle of civilization is about five thousand to seven thousand years old. These statements are presented today as facts in the face of evidence of a society that built a twenty-acre complex that reliably dates to at least eleven thousand if not fourteen thousand years ago.

The official story at this point can be characterized as nothing other than blatant disinformation. As a sidebar, let me remind you that from about 1600 through the 1900s Christian theology taught that the entire universe was created in one week in the year 4004 BCE. It's interesting that the official position of learned scientists still informs us that civilization is merely a few thousand years old—not so different from the age of the universe as espoused by official church dogma. Is this a coincidence?

My ultra-thinking leads me to conclude the Christian church laid the foundation for the belief innocently enough, and scientists simply became so invested in the story regarding the progression of humanity that they can't get themselves out of it without losing face. Again, the religion of science ends up promoting certain sets of beliefs that often have little if any basis in reality. As is my opinion with regard to advanced technology, I think many anthropologists appreciate that the narrative promoted by science is at best a half-truth if not patently false. Still, as is the case regarding the Big Bang theory of the cosmos, for various reasons they choose to conform to the dogma of science, assuming we are weak-minded thinkers who defer to their betters.

Societies of cooperating people don't simply pop up. They evolve over hundreds if not thousands of years, and as they do, they develop advanced technology. Should the mysteries of the Great Pyramid, Machu Picchu and Göbekli Tepe, be openly and honestly evaluated without the bias of dogmatic fog, we could appraise objective evidence in support of refreshed ideas. Absent plausible ideas from the smartest among us, we're left to think for ourselves. Since I value the simple process of ultra-thinking, let me formally thank our archeologists and anthropologists for being ideologues and spurring my mind in retort.

Part II

PHILOSOPHICAL ULTRATHOUGHTS

Now that you have a clear understanding of what it means to ultra-think in hopes of producing Ultrathoughts, let's delve further into philosophy and metaphysics. This is the part of the book where I start to get deeply personal, and in doing so, unfortunately, feathers of some may be ruffled a bit. Candidly, my friends may abandon me when I dare to speak honestly of topics like the Godhead. I am a fully-integrated member of Western society, a society that has a dominant, over-arching view of God. My understanding doesn't conform to that opinion and may be considered a blasphemous view by some. Though I remind myself that no one is forced to share their very personal opinion of the spiritual, I shall do so in my attempt to encourage you to ultra-think. Just keep in mind the intent of Ultrathoughts is not to solve the world's problems but to engage your entire brain, thereby contributing to your own well-conceived truth. I shall now delve further into my forbidden philosophy.

CHAPTER 11

MIND, BRAIN, AND SOCIETAL TRUTH

Most of us believe the mind of an individual is tied somehow to the physical brain. I assume this is true, and though the mind could be a "thing," our mind doesn't express itself absent the brain, at least initially. Of course, as of this date, we can't definitively say the mind is anything other than a meta idea. Still, our minds appear to be a dominant facet of our life. Setting aside any detailed analysis of this unsolvable mind-brain paradox concerning who's the leader of the duo, let's acknowledge there exists a kind of feedback loop where the brain and mind work together to accomplish both shared and selfish objectives.

We must limit our scope when ultra-thinking overly complex subjects, so we'll reduce the issue of mind versus brain to some fundamentals. First, we should clarify the difference between an individual and a person. An individual represents a purely physical being. A person, on the other hand, is the essence of self that may or may not include the physical body of an individual. For example, President George Washington is a person, an idea, but he was also an individual who lived two hundred and thirty years ago. The person we perceive as him is all that matters to us today.

We understand that the brain exists regardless of the mind. The brain is purely physical. While it's open to honest debate whether the mind exists at all, let's assume the mind of an individual is an actual thing. Still, in order for an individual to access the mind, a physical brain must be engaged, acting as a tool or receiver. Therefore, it stands to reason for purposes of this line of ultra-thinking that the brain is primary. The brain can exist without the mind, but the mind can't be accessed by the individual without the brain.

Although the mind can exhibit a spiritual nature, this is not always the case. Many are of seemingly sound mind, yet they appear to have no spiritual inclination. If the mind is not required to always express a spiritual nature, though the mind is most likely meta (non-physical) it can't be considered a spiritual part of the Godhead. Still, we keep coming back to recognize that through engagement and mastery of the brain, the mind does often manifest a spiritual nature—or at least the mind serves as a conduit between the physical (the brain) and the spiritual realm of the Godhead.

The amount of research regarding questions dealing with topics concerning mind-brain interaction and some sort of spiritual connections is overwhelming. There are literally hundreds of thousands of new pages written annually, and you should be reminded that few if any of these pages are likely to be authenticated through accepted scientific methods. Nevertheless, it is still worthwhile to note that cutting-edge research using new science hints at some strange relationships between the mind, the brain, and the unexplained forces that seem to exist in the cosmos. While traditional scientists may scoff at the direction of such research, a defender of new science need only remind a traditional cosmologist that he or she can't even tell us what makes up ninety percent or more of the universe. Any disparagement of the new by the old, with respect to this subject at least, is a hollow position to take. It is entirely possible that as more sensitive equipment is developed, new cutting-edge science may one day be able to document that our individual minds are not only a product of the physical organ of the brain but are specifically influenced by the fundamental energy present throughout the universe.

Certain researchers believe their investigations are bolstering ideas regarding the presence of not only an individual mind but also of a collective mind, or CM for short. Many ancient philosophers held similar opinions, though most never agreed with each other. Researchers today likewise differ in their opinion of the purported nature of this CM.

Some believe the CM is merely a sort of mathematical average of the collective group of individual minds, while others are confident the CM is a specific type of meta thing. Other investigators trust CM will be proven to act independently and of its own self-created volition. This is the line of ultra-thinking that seems to reflect concepts of world soul that were so often considered by the very first philosophers. The CM, in the vein of world soul, would then be considered distinct and possibly superior to the individual soul. By implication, the CM is then superior to the mind of man.

As with all other metaphysical concepts, all truth regarding these ideas exist outside the bounds of objectivity. The existence of a collective mind, individual mind, and even the Godhead are entirely unsupported by proof of a physical nature. As a result, you either believe or you don't.

While considering the CM, let's briefly contemplate cultural differences in belief. Belief in a CM and world soul is not common in Western culture. Cultures of the East and West both tend to believe in the individual mind but differ in their acceptance of a belief in a CM. Truth, faith, and belief are very often localized to a region of the globe. An obvious way to prove the statement is the simple definition of cold.

"Cold" to someone residing in the jungles of Ecuador is far different from "cold" to one who has lived their lifetime in Iceland. Residents of each location have incorporated an understanding of their definition, or truth, of "cold." Truth is often nothing other than common agreement. This concept of localized truth infers that truth itself is subject to its own unique domain of applicability.

We are each a product of our surroundings. Throughout this series of books, I have spoken of the influence of the mind of society or *MOS* for short. The MOS expresses inertia in favor of what is considered a worthy truth. Society favors and tacitly validates belief. Ideas or themes of child-rearing, god-worship, manner of dress, and even language spoken are set by MOS. The dominant societal myth in the West doesn't usually incorporate concepts of world soul or collective mind; therefore, many like me have not accepted these views. Certainly, we each create our own story, but we should not deny that we do so within context of a culture. Absent intent to act otherwise we will be a product of our society. I recognize many readers may have made said break, but I have not.

The MOS is a dominant influencer of mind. It exists to a varying degree in any group intelligent life which needs to cooperate. For example, take a pack of wolves. Wolves recognize the leader of the pack. That leader may or may not be the strongest or best fighter of the group but until the MOS of the pack expresses a weak tone that leader is assumed worthy of the title. The MOS is a malleable force. It doesn't actively do anything. It only seems to accept or deny the validity of a truth.

The force of MOS is appreciated by many of us as a kind of societal, or peer pressure in favor of a particular theme or group opinion. The MOS, just as any club or church, indoctrinates new members into a certain way of thought not through "action" but through this often very subtle pressure. When an individual chooses to go against the group, the person experiences a type of psychological bullying. The noisiness of peers becomes a sort of arbiter of truth concerning what is a socially acceptable belief.

Note again, MOS, is not an intentional actor like CM or world soul. It exerts a presence or theme, but it is groups of individuals who are behind the force that seeks conformity. As the individual mind internalizes the truth of the group, the individual mind recalibrates its own beliefs. Individual mind-myth reviews the position of the MOS, gauges its inertia, and then adjusts its own myth accordingly. Individuals form opinions regarding what is fact, fantasy, lies, or honesty as they simultaneously battle the subtle force of indoctrination.

It is a fact that a strong tradition of belief embraced by society will not change without some monumental force. This principle explains why a strongly dogmatic society tends to last year after year, while a weak society—one whose citizens readily don't accept a standard set of beliefs or MOS—finds itself in constant turmoil. MOS always remains changeable because it is simply a theme. Weaken the societal myth, and societal values are in jeopardy. Once values are gone, the MOS will either change its dogma and attempt to stabilize once more or it will collapse. When a society experiences the loss of its fundamental beliefs, the dogma and quite possibly the society itself will end.

Although societies rarely collapse, eventually, they all will. Beliefs and values are under constant pressure to change. The primary pressure on the MOS results from individuals who, themselves, are products of personally evolving beliefs, truths, and values. If enough individuals or certain key influential citizens have internalized a new truth of their own myth of the mind, even long-held societal beliefs or truths could change. Such change experienced by the MOS may happen incrementally or suddenly.

Now that we have devoted some ultra-thinking to understanding the individual mind, CM, and MOS, let's circle back to further consider the physical brain. Most would say the mind is, first, reactive to the physical dictates of the brain. In book one, I spoke at length about our leaning toward either the logical-left or creative-right hemisphere. Each hemisphere is naturally inclined to think a certain way.

This innately biased organ, the brain, acts as a chief executive with the only password to the company database, though no biochemist or neurologist understands how. Sensory organs—eyes, ears, skin, tongue, etc.—gather information, and the brain in most cases decides what happens next. Sensory experiences are physical experiences. Therefore, much of the work the brain does is oriented toward physical or material stuff. Even the eyeballs are extensions of physical touch. The retina of the eye experiences the touch of photons of light, and the brain produces what we interpret as an image. This image is a product of the brain and exists only *in* the story of your mind. The image is an *idea*, not a physical thing. If you don't process the experience there is no idea of the image maintained. With that said, you are reminded that this image can be held within either your conscious or subconscious mind, so it is sometimes challenging to determine what actual information the brain chooses to process. If you still believe, as we were once taught, that the brain stores an actual image, like a JPG file, that theory has been debunked. The brain works to interpret experiences and builds patterns of neuron cells.

It is now believed by a substantial number of neurologists that even the word "memory" is a misnomer. Maybe we aren't remembering anything. We might be simply reconstituting a data interpretation on the fly. The information is what is being held within a pattern of cells, not the interpretation. This data is then used to create an interpretation or image through a real-time calculation. If this is true, we're not relying upon a pattern of neuron cells to remember an event. We are creating an organic reenactment facilitated by some as yet undiscovered brain function. The brain may be running some kind of organically derived algorithm with the mind being a kind of paragraph written based on the results.

I ultra-think the brain is doing a bit of both. Expressed as mind, brain sometimes interprets via a mental algorithm, and at other times it reads from its narrative. It retains impressions, but these are contextual. We often comprehend our past when we simply "read" from our mind-myth. Your brain is casually re-calculating based on current sensory input deemed relevant and or plausible. Brain rejects the implausible. The mind is lazy and prefers to read rather than think anew. Intentional thoughts can be derived, but it's not particularly easy to do. As a narrative becomes dense, the effort required to re-think increases. Occasionally, inexplicable meta forces from beyond seem to seek to influence the mind. Shield the mind from sensory input and meta influence and the mind will keep reading of its history. This creates an increasingly rigid narrative. Welcome influence or simply ultra-think and the person of you can change.

Effectively we are each a kind of formula or digital creation based on information that has been organized by mind in the form of a story presented in real time. Whether people know it or not, the person of today is a manifestation of a version of this story. The formula of you is created or recreated every second. I suggest that even after the body's passing the algorithmic recalculation of the person continues even without new information. I've started to seriously consider the idea that our person simply exists in an eternity at this very moment having neither past nor present, not unlike the nature of the timeless Godhead. Neither the formula nor its product, your *digital-self*, will change absent outside influence. When the individual that is your body passes, the formula repeats in the meta realm.

Is a type of *digital-self* a person of the cosmos unbound in its entirety? If so, it then makes sense that although digital-me exists in formula, I can't contemplate its presence while bound to the physical individual. Maybe I can't ever be two persons. While physical, I can only contemplate of the spiritual. While spiritual, I can only contemplate of the physical. That is worth ultra-thinking in more depth. Is that where the whole idea of reincarnation comes from? A *digital-self* continually recycling in the physical realm?

Consider the person we know as George Washington. The formula of the president has recalculated as a meta idea for over two hundred years. MOS, my children, and I have impressions of him based on the product of a formula. If I don't seek to consider specific revisions, I will simply accept the common formula accepted by the MOS. When the formula or the data changes—say for instance we find evidence that he was a crook—the person of him is new. Assuming I validate the new information, my impression of him will change. This rather innocuous event can urge further change, provided I consider the information plausible and relevant. For example, say I strive to model myself based on this "honest" president. When my impression of him changes, the person of me will then change. A meta impression of a man long since dead worked to influence a meta presentation of myself in real-time. We must then ask, "Is George Washington truly dead, or has his mortal existence simply passed away?"

Though we are a presentation, the ultimate meta-self, we are also physical individuals comprised of atoms that work in synchronicity for several decades. The physical body, of course, reacts to experiences of the brain, whether they are based on physical matter or mental delusion. When the body's own hand is being burned, the brain instructs the mouth to cry out in recognition of physical pain. The experience and the physical reaction to it are added to our story. The skin of the hand may even blister from the experience. As strange as it seems, there is debate as to what exactly is the root cause of the observed blistering. Is it:

- A purely physical reaction of the body, needing little or no brain interaction?
- A physical reaction managed by brain interaction, wherein the brain invokes the biology of the body to blister?
- Is it a mind-myth creation that spurs action by the biology of the body?

Evidence provided by science has traditionally-supported option number two: a physical reaction managed by the brain. The physical pain and the blistering of skin involve both brain interpretation and physical response to the physical experience of heat on the skin. Any medical doctor can tell you the chemical and biological process involved in the blistering of the skin. Nevertheless, sophisticated research tells us there is much more going on than basic biology.

It is a provable fact that biological reactions can be brought about simply by the belief of the mind (option three). In experiments, skin blistering can be brought about by the assumption of heat damage to the skin when in fact no heat exists. Experiments confirm that the brain or the mind somehow present the reality of a physical experience when there is no physical cause, not unlike the placebo effect. Once you begin to appreciate what your mind is capable of doing in partnership with the brain, you may be more likely to agree with my statement that what is important to our daily existence is merely a delusional reality or illusional truth of the mind.

Your mind-myth is in total control of your world. Certainly, the MOS and physical reality impact that narrative, but no one other than the person of you determines whether you smile or cry today. A starving child is laughing this very moment, as happy as

any human can be, while a person with every advantage imagin-
able is being pushed beyond the brink of despair. I suggest you
take a long deep breath, pause, and choose to smile.

CHAPTER 12

THE EXISTENCE OF ALIENS AND THE MOS

I t is a statistical certainty (extremely probable) that extraterrestrial life exists. Intelligent life does exist beyond; however, until the MOS accepts the idea as being more plausible than not we as a people will continue to deny this literal truth. Whether their existence is in the form of organic life, energy life force, or artificial life-forms, the statistics prove the point. Still, we are faced with the "Fermi paradox" described by Enrico Fermi. Fermi, a prominent physicist of the nuclear age, devoted countless hours of ultra-thinking to many topics. Only one of these still captures the attention of everyday people: Why do we see no signs of intelligence elsewhere in the universe? Or, to put it succinctly, where are they? Fermi had the mind to run the numbers.

He calculated that it should take five million to fifty million years to colonize a galaxy similar to our own Milky Way. If there are calculated to be roughly two hundred billion galaxies in total containing more than two trillion stars (more stars than grains of sand on planet Earth), without statistical doubt there has been ample opportunity for alien life to interact with Earth.

The explanations for the paradox are many. The more common include:

1. Extraterrestrials would find it far more efficient to transfer information than physical matter. Why send actual alien beings or spaceships when something like a small space probe can do the job remotely? Therefore, after the first explorers millions of years ago encountered our solar system, the creatures simply chose to monitor us remotely.

2. Intelligent life and their civilizations are still too far away in space and time. Stars and galaxies are incredible distances apart. To simply run a probability analysis without an appreciation of the vast distance bound by some semblance of passing time misses the point of the question. They still haven't had time to get here.

3. All life, biological or artificial, is subject to the risk of extinction or at least decimation. Civilizations of intelligent life are often destroyed by things like supernovas, meteors, you name it.

4. Very few if any intelligent species have arisen. Fermi may have statistically proven intelligence but not truly advanced intelligence necessary for interstellar travel. After all, great apes have existed on earth for millions of years, and life for possibly three billion years or more; but even we can barely leave the solar system and can't yet fathom leaving the galaxy with even our most advanced space probes.

The list goes on and on. Explanations in response to Fermi will continue to be promoted, argued, and revamped until the inertia of public opinion changes.

Today, though many say they believe there is intelligent life elsewhere, few have actually devoted ultra-thinking to this extremely complex question. As a result, even believers vacillate in their response when pressured. As we've learned, the question today is framed in terms of theoretical math. Why? Because we look to science to validate or provide objective proof in support of our beliefs. But why should we assume every single question needs to be proven by scientific evidence? This premise is the problem.

Science can't answer every question for the individual. Whether you believe it or not, none of us know any more than our mind-myth validates. Ultimately, you and I either accept or deny the existence of intelligent life beyond our planet. Truth is self-created. Still, we must admit that the mind of society influences our willingness to validate any truth. I ultra-think that sophisticated extraterrestrial life exists, but society would still call me a fool. Therefore, I risk my reputation by stating my truth in an open forum. Most people don't choose to be called foolish by the masses, so it is commonly left to MOS to determine whether revolutionary ideas like intelligent life elsewhere are a fact or fantasy.

Many who believe in alien life elsewhere and similar strange themes scoff at my dependence on statistics and logic. They don't need math from dead physicists like Fermi to justify or offer support of their truth that life or intelligent life exists beyond. Furthermore, they are fearless in their willingness to be considered foolish by the MOS. Believers across the planet just seem to know in their gut that extraterrestrial life exists, or they've had personal experiences that offer adequate validation of their mind-myth. Advocates of this belief consider the existence to be a plain fact or truth supported by ample physical proof. Some even believe their facts are supported through objective science and that the masses are being deceived and not shown this evidence.

This particular question provides a very vivid example of the power of one's delusional reality. Believe in extraterrestrials or not; the choice is yours. Regardless of your choice today, I believe that eventually the MOS will be moved by the weight of enough individuals to change its opinion with regard to life beyond. When this happens, the MOS will have created a revised view of reality and will accept alien life as fact, and individual minds will change as a result.

Recently, scientists have begun to accept the idea that the building blocks for organic life are not unique to our planet. I suggest that it's merely a question of time until the MOS will expand its belief to include acceptance of the truth of extraterrestrial life. For argument's sake, let's assume I'm correct, and alien life does exist outside our planet. In such case the absolute physical reality is that 'creatures' from beyond do exist this very day, but the MOS has not yet recognized that fact. Let's further assume some type of intelligent life could or even has already arrived on Earth. They may be here at this moment, but the inertia of the MOS is so inclined to deny a change of belief that it denies this fact in the face of actual objective evidence.

I'm not confident that most of us could necessarily even comprehend the difference between objective evidence of aliens and no objective evidence. I assume forms of life across the universe are not bound to our commonly accepted preconceptions of the topic. Life is not bound to the conceptions of our delusion. Just as I can't fully comprehend the spiritual, I believe we can't comprehend all life in the universe. Regardless of the validity of this line of ultra-thinking, there certainly appears to be significant misinformation surrounding the topic of aliens. Is this to be expected given the nature of the subject matter, or is the misinformation spread for a purpose? Do societal leaders wish to keep the broader population in the dark about alien life?

Regardless of objective proof of their existence or whether misinformation is being spread, if an extraterrestrial presence existed on our planet, what would the creatures actually do? Any interaction between us and an alien creature or their intelligence might be best predicted by considering how our brightest individuals behave when among an "inferior" species.

The most intelligent humans on our planet have not typically exploited their advantage for material success. Very smart people are often disinterested in material substance or in obtaining control over the masses. The most intelligent seem to be content to observe and contemplate rather than seek an advantage. It occurs to me that the brightest among us tend to live an austere or ascetic existence. Furthermore, they seem to act toward others with a light touch, almost like passive researchers. How would an intelligent *H. sapiens*, say an expert in the field of biology, interact with alien life? Without an agenda to conquer, she will generally observe and respect, taking in the beauty of the observed life. One without an overactive ego is perfectly content to let others be themselves.

Now let's consider how a group of humans would interact with a different race or foreign intelligence. The mind of society often develops inertia from individuals who are overtly ego-driven. The MOS is then expressed as a relatively obnoxious presence. A few trouble-makers in the group guide the behavior of the collective. In such a case, being scrutinized by a different group, the observed alien in my example may quickly find itself in mortal danger and be forced to protect its interest. The MOS often sinks to the lowest common denominator of the group. Often that lowest set of values is based on self-interest. A united group of individuals seeking an ego-driven advantage is a powerful force, quickly overtaking any single individual. While the intelligent individual tends to rise to his or her full potential, the tone of the MOS is unpredictable at best. Historically, civilizations seem to have sought conquest of others.

This appears to be a fundamental aspect of our species and other social pack animals. An individual dog might be curious, playful, or angry, but a pack of dogs confronting another pack will immediately gauge whether they have an opportunity. If they can, they will take the advantage. If not, they will run or hide.

A handful of individuals could probably act pleasantly when faced with alien life-forms. On the other hand, if our whole human race encounters an extraterrestrial race, I assume there would be a high chance of confrontation. Since I believe in alien life and believe there is a significant chance certain power brokers can confirm my suspicion, I'm left to ultra-think the dynamic. Quite possibly the reason we are given no objective proof of aliens is that leaders within our society are protecting us, and the strange creatures from ourselves.

CHAPTER 13

THERE IS NO CONSPIRACY

The idea of a conspiracy by evil men holding us back has a certain appeal. We are thinking and well-meaning people, so if society isn't improving, something or someone must be working against our noble attempts. If we see no actual enemy, then why does it appear we're having to fight to maintain a peaceful and moral existence?

In mathematics, you may be familiar with the concept of the lowest common denominator, or LCD for short. The best way to describe this idea is to determine what is the most basic common feature, number, or element of a set. For instance, regarding organic life, one might say the LCD is a carbon molecule. Another example: If you have a group of people standing in line at a coffee shop, what fundamental characteristic do they all share? You may say they are all standing. I would go lower and say they all want something from the store. The point is, what is a base characteristic unique amongst the set? LCD is a concept that reminds us that when a group of individuals congregates, very often only their commonalities remain discernable—just as when you view a beach you don't see the multicolored grains of sand. You just see a dominant allover tan color, the LCD.

Our Western society is an amalgamation of countless values. Because society is focused on material pursuits to the benefit of the individual, our common values tend to center on themes of power, control, and money. In modern societies of the West, we tend to live a mostly secular, non-spiritual existence. As a result, the MOS has incorporated a weak sense of morality. Not to say the MOS has no inertia in favor of moral behavior—we're not rioting in the streets—but our morals are rather weak and inconsistent. This makes it unlikely that high moral standards would be the lowest common characteristic of our group. When we blend the societal influences of business, government, spiritual individuals, secularized individuals, and countless organizational groups in Western society, the LCD would probably be something along the lines of a quest for more money or power.

I suggest these types of LCDs—money and power—appear to the individual as the enemy fighting against the person in his or her moral quest. Philosophically, this evil enemy has frequently been characterized as a type of demonic force—sometimes even personified as the Devil. Today the MOS of our secular society has substituted terms like "big business," "big brother," or even specific individuals for our concept of the evil Devil.

The innate predisposition of our mind seeks to explain what we perceive as evil by intention. Furthermore, recall that the individual, being raised in Western society, would have built a delusional reality that assumed the individual is superior to the group. When he or she attempts to explain the world they see— the LCDs of money and power—the mind constructs a story. The adaptation to one's narrative upon considering the ongoing war of good and evil is to naturally see this as a conspiracy against the individual. The mind of a person has narcissistic tendencies and is led to believe this fight is the result of a conspiracy of evil actors. There is no fight. There is no conspiracy.

CHAPTER 14

THERE IS NO HELL, BUT ALL DOGS GO TO HEAVEN

N o one individual can be credited with the philosophical origin of heaven and hell. Generally, Heaven is considered a
place of everlasting bliss, and Hell everlasting torment. These
"places" are considered in the mind as being either meta concept
or physical location. Despite the nature of the places, they are
usually thought of as everlasting locations for the soul after the
death of a physical body. Of course, we all don't agree on our nuance of interpretation. Still, I'm quite confident that most don't
consider Heaven and Hell to be specific physical places today.

If you have accepted the idea of the soul in your personal
views, you probably also have some opinion on Heaven and Hell.
I surmise that your current belief is basically a reflection of your
upbringing. Our society generally feeds us a narrative about the
afterlife, and most of us don't give the idea much serious thought.
Frankly, to do so risks undermining your entire set of spiritual
beliefs about the Godhead.

Evidence indicates our species has considered an afterlife experience for 50 thousand to 150 thousand years. Other hominins
may have done so even earlier. There have been many variations
of concepts similar to heaven and hell expressed by humanity.
Regardless of era or specific interpretation, we create a delusional
reality or illusional truth of mind, and once it is established, most
people don't rethink their view of the afterlife. Just as was the case
of our consideration of the death penalty in book one, *Intentional*

Thought, it is much easier to reflexively adopt a view than to honestly contemplate this type of heavy subject.

In this chapter, I'm describing my Ultrathoughts within the context of terms commonly used in Western society, but as you've read in book two, *Godhead Designs*, heaven and hell are not Christian ideas per se. We believe that, at least as far back as the dynastic Egyptians, the ideas existed. It is believed by some that the Egyptians were the very first to conceive of Hell as an actual place of the underworld. They used different terms, but funerary texts refer to a literal place of Hell, a concept of hell, and even a version of a Devil. Were these the very first? We'll never know for sure.

With regard to Christian beliefs, we can credit Augustine and later Renaissance artists for solidifying a very common view that there are actual physical locations for Heaven and Hell. Believers even today are indoctrinated to think of Christianity literally, but they are not banned from the religion if they think otherwise.

The literal version of belief has coexisted with the far older interpretations of heaven and hell as concepts for more than one thousand years. Many still believe in locations, and Christian dogma seems to promote the idea of places; however, in our modern mechanized society, even devout Christians find it difficult to conceive of an underworld and glorious Heaven in the sky. Christian beliefs evolved from a meta concept to more of a physical location and then back to meta belief. In Christian and even Jewish theology, the entire issue is quite muddled. Although Christian theology demands the acceptance of some form of an afterlife for the soul, and the Jewish religion is far more flexible, most sects of these religions allow believers to believe whatever specific interpretation they choose regarding the resting place of the soul.

Today the view of the MOS concerning this topic is somewhat weak, but things are rapidly changing. The MOS currently allows people to individually validate their own view regarding the final resting place of the soul as a statement of fact or faith, provided the individual doesn't advertise their belief with enthusiasm. From my view, if an individual finds comfort by believing in places like Heaven or Hell, what is the harm?

I doubt the MOS will allow one to believe as they wish much longer. The broader society will very soon shun those who have a belief deemed wholly irrational, a belief in physical places. I further suggest that eventually, the entire concept of heaven and hell will be rejected across the board. MOS is evolving in favor of a denial of any spiritual belief.

With regard to my own Ultrathoughts I choose to believe we are each in our own meta type of heaven or hell today, not simply in the afterlife. Believing that the essence or soul of the person exists beyond the physical, the state one occupies today will likely be the state they occupy after their physical body ceases to breathe. I see no reason the naïve, the innocent, and people of limited mental capability couldn't occupy a heaven of sorts. The default position of the spiritual is brotherly love. Absent intent, the default remains; souls reside in a type of heaven.

Furthermore, I'm inclined to see no malice in the essence or spirit of my dog, cat, and even the pet skunk I had as a twelve-year-old child. From my point of view, all dogs are in heaven today. Assuming they have a soul, that soul would rest in timeless bliss. Whether any of my belief is offered support by objective science is irrelevant. What matters is the belief validated. I choose to believe dogs, the infirmed, and the mentally ill are all—and will stay—in a state of heaven.

Let's now delve deeper into the life, journey, or even after-life of the soul. Unlike the body, it is certainly plausible that the soul wouldn't exist in time and space. The world of the physical wouldn't bind the spiritual soul, so I have further confirmation that the physical places of Heaven and Hell don't make any sense. Conceptually, heaven and hell are absolutely meta in my mind. I also think it is very likely that a soul experiences these states for eternity regardless of having a physical partner or not. My soul then exists in either heaven or hell at this very moment and may or may not even appreciate its physical partner, my earthly body.

At the physical death of my body, my soul does one of two things: 1) Seeks to be near or rejoin the Godhead, experiencing bliss if successful and less than bliss if not. 2) It reincarnates to bind with another life-form and continues to recycle for eternity living in a state of heaven or hell periodically. I lean toward the first option, but don't categorically reject the second.

We will never have clear physical proof of either of my suppositions. I choose to consider each plausible, though I consider the first more plausible. I assume all life has a chance to reside in a heaven now and forever. Even though I admit my views, still I recognize my Ultrathoughts concerning the destiny of the soul are weak. The issue will always remain beyond my mortal brain and mind to fully comprehend. I don't think I can truly fathom the mind of God but I like to try nonetheless.

My leaning toward the first idea is probably a remnant of my left-leaning brain and Western upbringing. Had I been raised in India, I'm confident I would believe option two is more likely. Had I been born in dynastic Egypt, I would have believed something entirely different. With that admission, I don't have a problem continually validating my own imprecise perception. Any answer, for me, is far better than no answer. This belief in the journey of the soul reconciles nicely with my belief in the Trinitarian philosophy of God. If I will never perfect any truth, this truth will do.

Further ultra-thinking informs me that the soul always seeks the pure love of God. This desire is why we humans seem to feel the presence of God deep within. We are all naturally-born seekers, again a unique aspect of our species. To deny our seeking instinct would be to deny that which makes us human. Of course, the desire of the soul is often thwarted by physical action and influence as well. If the soul is not nurtured and encouraged by its physical partner it is likely to fail. Such unintentional failure may describe a "sleeping" soul—a concept often referred to in spiritual texts to which I give credence. A sleeping soul could also be that of a person who "believes" in a God but doesn't contemplate the fate of a soul in an afterlife.

The concept of the punishment of the sleeping soul encourages us to believe in a metaphysical hell or even a physical place of Hell. As I ultra-think subjects like manifest evil, and what it actually means to be anti-God, it becomes apparent that the sleeping soul may reside in a hell even if it is not "evil." Hell is certainly not a place and does not need to be a state of torment; it is merely a state not in harmony with God. I think of a hellish existence as a state of being absent any sincere quest for the pure love of God. A soul that "sleeps" in this context probably wouldn't be in heaven, so I would assume it would be in a hellish state. With that said, if the person seeks the love of God while living, it's plausible that said soul exists in a heavenly state. Assuming a soul exists postmortem, the sleeping soul, like any other, would reside for eternity in whatever state it was in at the passing of the body.

Expanding my ultra-thinking further, what would happen to an absolutely vacant soul? A soul immersed in a physical reality but having no spiritual inclination? I warned you about my forbidden philosophy, so let's cut to the chase: what happens to the soul of a naturalist or an agnostic at death? Notice I left atheists out of the above consideration. An atheist may have some sort of spiritual belief; it is merely different than your own.

Let's start with the easy part of the question. What happens to the soul of a naturalist, a thinking individual who categorically rejects the Godhead? This person is an a-spiritual *H. sapiens*. I think that their soul is in hell today and for all eternity. If my statement was too harsh, be reminded that my position is not offensive to a true naturalist. They don't believe any of this stuff anyway. Besides, I don't judge. I'm merely answering a question.

The fate of an agnostic's soul is far more interesting to ponder. A self-admitted agnostic is a person who allows at least a faint contemplation of the Godhead within their mind, while a naturalist has made a conscious decision to deny any possibility. This is a difference of grave importance with regard to my Ultrathoughts. The agnostic is not spiritually vacant but spiritually doubting. I don't ultra-think the soul of an agnostic is necessarily a neglected or sleeping soul. I think there is a pretty good chance the soul of an agnostic typically resides in heaven provided the person actually seeks rather than neglects the Godhead. On the other hand, an agnostic too immersed or distracted in the physical realm to bother to seek would probably be "rewarded" with that same level of apathy by the Godhead. The soul of an agnostic probably shifts between heaven and hell quite often.

I do ultra-think the final decision regarding the fate of the soul is the absolute prerogative of the Godhead. Just as I can choose what to believe as my truth, God may choose what soul is in heaven or hell at the passing of the body. *H. sapiens* are special creatures, and agnostics just may be the poor souls so often referred to in spiritual texts. God may have absolute pity for the agnostic. In my review of material consolidated in book two, I couldn't help but notice that the spiritual thinker walks a thin line between agnosticism (i.e., confusion) and belief. When they dare to ultra-think their God, that struggle seems to be occasionally rewarded by the Godhead with an Ultrathought but doubt frequently returns. As a result, they may be the ultimate benefactors of the pure love of God. To struggle with belief is to be blessed with the guidance of the Holy Spirit as a sign of the love of the Godhead. Therefore, it may be the agnostic and not the fervent believer who is truly right before God.

As odd as this may strike the reader, I don't believe heaven in concept is "good" and hell is "bad" in our common use of the terms. The bliss of heaven is our natural state, which is why it is our goal to stay there. The idea that a soul becomes irrelevant and resides in hell, with regard to the Godhead, is actually far worse than "bad" or any expression of the negative. It is, in fact, a cosmic tragedy that should be considered a hell beyond expression. Just try to imagine the emptiness of truly being irrelevant to any and everything. This is the true opposite of love: to live for eternity in a state of irrelevance. Such an absolute waste of potential should cause a pit in your stomach. This would be a complete failure of the soul. More to the point, it is a failure of the soul's mortal partner who failed to keep his or her soul in heaven.

CHAPTER 15

THE NEEDS OF THE ONE OUTWEIGH THE MANY

I don't believe world soul or collective mind (CM) exists. There-fore, from my perspective God has merely one entity to be concerned with, the individual soul. Each soul is unequivocally equal and infinitely valuable. Those who subscribe to the con-cept of world soul would probably disagree with this core basis of my philosophy. In their view the individual soul is not the most important thing to the Godhead presence. That title belongs to world soul, or no particular thing at all.

Given my perspective, I note an inherent flaw of spiritual collectivism and all political systems of societal governance be they democracy, socialism, or communism. A government ruling a large group of people will render any individual meaningless. An individual being burdened is of very little importance when weighed against the benefit to the collective. There may be no sin-ister intent behind a collectivist action but the statement stands; governments are anti-God. Conversely, God is only concerned about the single soul and has no regard for the group as a collec-tive.

Let's consider this dynamic more thoroughly and truly at-tempt to understand why every single person is of equal and in-finite value to the Godhead. The individual, unlike the MOS, possesses the potential to build a special relationship with the spiritual Godhead through a human soul. The Godhead, being pure love, welcomes the relationship and values every single soul as much as a collective of countless souls. For God, there is no concept similar to "The needs of the many outweigh the needs of the few." Frankly, the phrase "needs of the many" is only applicable in the context of the physical realm, because there is no relevant equivalency to God. God doesn't view us as a collective, ever. God doesn't take votes of souls, count numbers, or weigh public opinion.

The MOS, of course, is soulless and will never have a spiritual relationship with the Godhead. While an individual can act in an anti-God manner, society is inherently and purely anti-God in all circumstances, not because of evil, but because it has no soul. Although the MOS can reflect goodness, the MOS will never reconcile to the Godhead and speaks for no soul.

The MOS is always an amalgamation of individual minds possessing inertia. It could express an inertia valuing faith, promoting specific traditions that encourage the worship of God. Inertia, a force, can only express its self-interest. The MOS could not exhibit a brotherly love to anyone or anything. It then follows that some individual somewhere would most likely fall outside the ideas supported by the MOS. Consequently, the MOS will burden at least one individual through the expression of its inertia. Therein lies the key. The need of the one must be superior to that of the collective group.

The preceding account is not a political Ultrathought. You'll note it is fundamentally anti-government altogether in defense of the spiritual nature of an individual person. While I may believe some government is necessary and some forms of government are better than others, all are oppressive to the spiritual sense of the person. We need a government to live in a society, and I agree with some who say that a constitutional republic is the least offensive form.

Part III

CHAPTER 16

ULTRATHOUGHTS ON GOD AND RELIGION

Whether it is a Christian church or a Buddhist temple, for me specifically, established religion just doesn't work. I ultra-think God worship is a personal experience. Furthermore, because all texts, ceremony, tradition, and rules have been written by humans, I believe that none is from the 'breath of God.' I don't value them more than my own judgement. Still, I do appreciate the value of text and tradition for their benefits to society. Where my views and statements can become confusing is that I am a self-professed Christian which implies my membership in the religion. I call myself that simply because the term is associated with the Trinitarian concept of God to which I subscribe. In jest I would call my "religion" the Origen-Luther sect of Christianity. It will only have one member, me.

As I describe my own Godhead design and archive my philosophy, keep in mind that I write to give you some ideas to ponder, not to advance my own views. At one point I was going to write this book anonymously, simply to avoid arguing points of religion with those who disagree. Upon reflection, I decided I must be fearless to be true to myself. We manifest the form of God we deem worthy in our mind, so if I am afraid to speak of my God, do I have one at all?

It will help you understand my position on religion if you are reminded of a couple of points driven home constantly in the Ultrathoughts Tripartite. We each create our own unique view, and that perspective is a delusional reality. I don't think we live in a matrix of holographic simulation. I could, but I could also train my mind to believe the world rests on the back of a giant turtle. So, if I'm going to train my mind, why not train it to think in a way that harmonizes with both my physical reality in Western society, and the ideas of brotherly love espoused by the Christian prophet Jesus of Nazareth? Today I elect to pursue a pleasant physical existence while ultra-thinking there is more for me beyond. The whole thing is a conscious choice. I am not simply a victim of life; I am a visionary creator of a person who exists today and will exist in the future.

My existence is a balancing act between attempts to keep my soul in heaven as I judiciously participate in a physical reality. Some days I do a better job than others. I am a work in progress, continuously creating a formula that I hope will be considered worthy before God. If indeed I am a victim of a flawed mind today, an infidel you choose to hate, a dupe of Satan, or a pawn used by a tribe of evil robots, simply know my mistake was very well intentioned. I choose my truth and while yours may fascinate me or possibly even enlighten my own view, it truthfully makes no difference to the person that I have created.

CHAPTER 17

PARTNER OF THE BODY

For a moment, think of the Godhead or the presence of God as a borderless cloud enveloping all, be it known or unknown. Photons of light are dispersed like poppy seeds throughout this cloud. Each of these photons or seeds represents a soul not yet partnered with a living person. The living presence of you is fundamentally a field of energy being composed of the primary energy of your specific material matter. To that energy and material of atoms, a soul becomes a partner. At such an event, the living being has both a spiritual and physical presence. The person is then whole. He or she is a soul partnered with a physical human.

God is the creator of all laws but need follow none. Both your physical and spiritual presence are subject to all of God's laws. Your physical part of matter, the human body, is subject to the laws of physics. Your vaporous field-like presence is likewise subject to the laws of God, though we do not understand these laws. Laws may overlap the realms in ways only understood by God. We may contemplate the spiritual and, even more specifically, God. As long as we are bound to a physical or material presence, any contemplation is fleeting as we constantly struggle to remain focused on the Godhead while being immersed in the physical.

To be you and to be aware of self is not only an indication that the spiritual and the physical are bound, but the individual can act with intent to influence this dual nature. The spiritual self acts with this awareness to communicate with the Godhead. To be human is to be different from any other life-form of which we are currently aware. Souls may or may not be unique to man.

Other life, or even all matter, may have a type of soul. But, I believe soul-initiated intent to seek God is a unique aspect of the human soul.

Science concludes there may be some self-awareness in the womb, but to truly become self-aware is a growth process. To be a living organism is to experience the pairing of the spiritual and physical, a process that must occur before the ability to act with intent is achieved. One can only develop self-awareness of the spiritual through maturity. On our planet today, I ultra-think this is the exclusive domain of humanity.

Prior to that transitional state of true maturation or growth of awareness, one could be said to exist as a naïve child. This is neither good nor bad. The naïve show no intent to neglect or dishonor the spiritual, and the default position of the human soul is to reside in a heavenly state of being. Heaven is not earned as much as it is lost. The naïve neither pleases nor disappoints God.

As a spiritual nature develops, knowledge is gleaned. The individual continues further interaction with the material world. We naturally become burdened. As we live in the physical, the human soul becomes laden with physical stress and the distractions of the world. This makes it challenging to focus on a spiritual connection to God. Quite possibly, these pressures are best managed if one limits material pursuits and puts the mind to the spiritual and immaterial. It is certainly obvious that the most spiritually enlightened are those who limit the indulgence of material desires. The human experience is ultimately a balancing act. Live a prosperous and productive physical existence all the while generating an expression of brotherly love in hopes of keeping the soul in a heavenly state.

In times of true stress, we note many seem to lose focus while others seem to thrive. Some become rather common animals. Survival instincts kick in. This is not by definition evil or bad; we are merely non-deferential to God when we become common. Unfortunately, this lack of focus may cause our soul to "fall" from heaven.

The Godhead never harbors any malice and continues to offer all that will be accepted. The Godhead has unyielding love for all creations. Yet we should understand that an individual who fails to master the soul in a manner harmonious with the universe and the spiritual realm of the Godhead is not fostering a productive relationship with the spiritual. To neglect the soul is to risk negating the unique benefits of being human. It is likely that we play a specific role in driving our soul to reunify with the Godhead. If we fail to guide our soul, can we really assume God would bother to intercede?

When the physical body is in distress, whether from injury or mental anguish, individuals often seem to seek a connection to God. While this tendency may be innate, if a person has neglected his or her spiritual ability for nearly a lifetime could they productively summon such a connection under duress? Isn't it fair to assume a mind that was never trained to contemplate the spiritual would be more challenged to successfully summon a spiritual connection than a mind that was well disciplined? Furthermore, people who only seek the comfort of the Godhead relationship during stressful times might eventually build an unfortunate Pavlovian dynamic. One who only knows God during stress might tend to associate the presence only with negative emotion. This would be particularly unfortunate because, as you know, God is the ultimate source of love and bliss.

This brings me to an Ultrathought regarding humanity's relationship with God. It is interesting that Christian philosophy and liturgy stress a curious premise: "The meek shall inherit the earth." Upon ultra-thinking the very nature of God and our unique ability to have a relationship with God while living in the material world, individuals will comprehend the phrase in its nuance. While we would generally agree that meek individuals may have as many or more stressors in their lives, they tend to be less likely to suffer the silent curse of physical or material pleasures. The curse of physical pleasures is the neglect of the soul. Stress leads one to seek God. This tendency is a good and valuable attribute if one seeks to build a deeper understanding of the spiritual realm. We only become our best through challenge. We are "antifragile" creatures, as noted author Nassim Taleb would say.

On the other hand, material distraction pleases the individual and distracts him or her from maintaining a spiritual connection. One who is content in the physical might grow to consider the spiritual unnecessary. To be clear, physical stuff or pleasures aren't inherently bad or good, but as is the case with all that is material, the physical is anti-God. Distractions of the physical tend to lead to failure of the soul because they lead the person to neglect the contemplation of God and soul.

CHAPTER 18

LOVE, LANGUAGE, TIME, AND GOD

The Godhead is a superhuman presence of pure love in my design. In the context of this section, love is probably best characterized as that of a parent who loves an innocent child; brotherly love. Beyond that it, He, or She is difficult to describe. He is not eternal since eternity contemplates time, and God exists outside of time and space. God simply *is*. My concept of God doesn't include consideration of judgment. God is not a punisher but a source of deep caring love. Regarding the Godhead, the spirit/theme of God is not good or positive in human terms. The concept of "good" is certainly better than "bad," yet I stress this does not apply when considering the Godhead.

I have no choice but to use language to express my particular concept. It's possible that this wasn't always the case. Conceivably ape-like humans a million years ago could communicate in depth without complex language, maybe they even used some sort of ESP, but that's not how we communicate in our era. Unfortunately, when it comes to the superhuman presence of God language must be used but it fails to communicate. Language is limiting and God is limitless.

To understand these statements is to appreciate why some creeds forbid producing an image or even a word in the representation of God. The image, being a flawed image of the perfect—as well as any word used to represent God—can't help but profane the subject. An appreciation of this idea is prevalent in many religions that forbid any image of God or his more important prophet(s). God shall not be defined within limits set by the mortal mind or material substance. "Time and space" and "good and bad" are examples of limitations that simply fail to adequately describe that which is truly of the spiritual realm. That which is spiritual defies any interpretation or limitation.

God is then best expressed only as the force of pure love—a love that is ill-defined by our common use of language. Just as we can't visually represent the presence of God, we find it difficult to adequately comprehend a loving presence through our language. This limitation unique to us in the physical realm is frustrating enough, but it is nearly unbearable when we observe that God has, apparently, acted in a manner which is bad, suboptimal, or even immoral. For instance, take the untimely death of a loved one. How could this be described through our language as a noble or proper act of a supposedly good and loving God? Honestly: it can't, and it won't be. The harsh truth is that often we simply need to move on. We must focus our minds on other issues rather than getting stuck in a feeble attempt to make sense of that which is patently inexplicable within the context of one's own mortal reality.

What we must understand is that our language falls short in our analysis. God is pure love, and that love so surpasses our concept of love that we cannot yet comprehend the comparison. God cannot be judged; therefore, God can never be deemed good or bad. God simply is. The thinker would be best served to ultra-think pure love rather than attempt to ultra-think the mind or acts of the Godhead.

CHAPTER 19

CHARITY MISUNDERSTOOD

Regarding concepts of the spiritual, the word "charity" creates a challenge. The word *Agape*, used in very early Greek translations of ancient texts has been translated and frequently interpreted as the highest form of selfless love. In crude use, it is also interpreted as synonymous with the word "charity," which in the language of old does not have the same meaning as it does for most of us today. In the original context, the translation of *agape* would be closer to a deep, heartfelt empathy than to our common perception of charity. Such retranslation infers a significantly different context from many biblical texts other than what we have been indoctrinated to believe.

It is important to remember that within the Jewish culture that permeated the lives of all biblical authors, charity was considered as much a type of tax as a true gift of the heart. Charity was a quasi-obligation for a Jew of the era; not quite the same thing as agape to a non-Jewish person.

Jewish society, being a subset of the broader civilization of the era, was basically self-supporting. That support, in terms of money or action, came from what was termed charity of the Jewish people. From a practical standpoint, it was virtually compulsory; nevertheless, it was called charity. Giving was a cultural obligation, part of being a Jew. This nuance is often lost when discussing charity, gifts, tithing, and the like, each of which is referenced in the Bible concerning the God of Abraham. In Western culture, when one reads that the Bible instructs or emphasizes the benefits of charity, we should keep this in mind and not automatically assume that it meant the giving of material goods or money out of the goodness of the heart. What it probably meant was to fulfill your civil responsibility and support the society for a variety of reasons in a number of ways.

To be charitable doesn't necessarily involve a material gift at all and certainly doesn't automatically indicate the gift is out of kindness. Charity—for the Jew, Christian, and Muslim individuals living millennia ago—was for all practical purposes a required tribute paid for being a member of the society. This distinction of meaning and interpretation was probably glossed over by church leaders as time passed. If believers in the faith came to consider agape to be an act of giving, rather than an emotional expression, leadership could take advantage of the ill-informed believer.

Charitable giving continues to be respectable for humanity, and it certainly is good for the individual recipient, but the act of giving charity itself is also good for the ego of the giver. Concerning interpretations of Christian philosophy, therein lies the challenge to an individual who wishes to perform a right deed.

Charitable giving, without restraint of ego, harms the spiritual soul of the giver as it simultaneously benefits the recipient. The action of giving, when done in a manner that recognizes the giver, will by its very nature suppress the giver's willingness to humble themselves before God. Giving, in and of itself, is not then a godly act. Ultra-thinking leads me to conclude that the only gift of worth to the soul of both the giver and the recipient is an anonymous gift given to a stranger. Such a gift would help the giver resist inflating the ego and would certainly help the recipient.

CHAPTER 20

RELIGION DOESN'T MEAN RELIGION

Before daring to ultra-think religion, we must start by appreciating that a spiritual philosophy of the Godhead exists separately from any religion. Religions are the children of philosophy; they may be presented as a general or specific representation of their parent. The important point is that within our narrative we should allow ourselves to contemplate the philosophy apart from the religion. Upon gaining an understanding of the philosophy, absent religious dogma, we can evaluate associated religions and any subsets of these religions, known as sects or denominations.

Now that we've clarified the difference between philosophy and religion, we must pause to appreciate regional perspectives. The word *religion* doesn't have a global definition; therefore, we must be careful to consider the culture from which the religion originated. Judeo-Christian values have been disseminated worldwide, but they haven't yet created a global MOS regarding spiritual beliefs. The culture and MOS of much of the globe are very different from that of Europe and the Americas. Consequently, there often exists a fundamental misunderstanding regarding the actual definition of the word religion. This hinders Ultrathoughts when attempting to contemplate the Godhead and specific religious dogma. To ultra-think on religion without an appreciation of this fact will create fundamentally flawed Ultrathoughts.

When we in the West use the word *religion*, we automatically isolate our thoughts to the Godhead, God, or the spiritual without any consideration of our specific culture or form of government. In fact, a colloquial definition of *religion* used in the West would be "a faith inclusive of a system of worship or dogma surrounding a superior force or presence." Notice this definition makes no mention of either culture or government. Religion is assumed to be a spiritual concept alone in the minds of most people.

An exception to this generalization may exist when one discusses Roman Catholicism, but even in this case, a discussion surrounding the authority of any government supposedly controlled by the Roman pope or Vatican City does not seriously consider the Roman Catholic Church to be a controlling authority regarding everyday societal governance. Even in the city of Rome itself, the seat of church leadership, the resident population is mostly secular, having little respect for official church edicts.

Such has been the case since the widespread adoption of a system of government that respects personal liberty. Promoted by John Locke in the 1700s as a key feature of any successful democratic government, this idea can be traced to earlier thinkers who sought to reform an overly dogmatic and self-interested Christian Church politic. Regardless of who gets credit, it happened. Led by the example set in the United States, today most Western societies whose cultures have Judeo-Christian roots have adopted the idea that the specifics of God worship need not be promoted by government. Church and state are two different things impacting the lives of citizens. To assume this separation of domains applies to any religion other than those of the Judeo-Christian family of faiths is a grave mistake. Virtually every other religion has bound itself directly to the ruling government to some degree.

This brings us to a discussion of religions common in India and the Eastern hemisphere of the globe inclusive of most of Asia. There are notable differences between Western philosophers in general and philosophers like Siddhartha Gautama Buddha of the East. Although each advocated a spiritual concept of the Godhead, philosophies of the West continued to evolve and ultimately segregated the spiritual from the physical realm culminating in concepts of Cartesian dualism. With that evolution came an emphasis on the individual soul and its specific journey post-mortality.

Eastern philosophy, although it doesn't necessarily deny the individual, leaves little doubt that the individual is of less importance than the collective group as a whole. The spiritual connectivity of the group, and concepts like world soul and collective mind, dominate the region of India and most of Asia. Certainly, ancient Hellenists contemplated similar philosophies. As specific Western concepts evolved post-Aristotle, they came to incorporate a vivid form of a particular God. This monotheistic tone took hold in the Mediterranean basin and overwhelmed views in support of a world soul. The MOS of Western culture became a fertile ground for acceptance of the God of Abraham. Concepts stressing the importance of the group fell outside the inertia of the MOS. Such was not the case in the MOS of Eastern culture. In Eastern culture and Eastern philosophy today, the group still takes precedence over the individual.

The most popular Western philosophies and their associated religions barely, if at all, consider a world soul. There is an obvious philosophical split between East and West. Godhead concepts of Western philosophy tend to stress a physical God with a spiritual nature, which fits nicely into a dualistic impression of reality. Those of the East tend to be oriented toward a universal view of world soul connectivity, a non-dualistic view of reality. The most popular religions on the globe, Christianity and Islam, specifically denounce the concept of a world soul. Followers, as a result, tend to view the issue of connectivity with skepticism. They stress the importance of the individual following God's will for his or her own benefit, much more than for the group.

Another obvious difference in fundamental religious dogma originating in East versus West is the issue of the soul's reincarnation. Historically, reincarnation concepts were quite common among the Hellenists of the West. Individual souls would usually if not endlessly recycle, but as religious dogma evolved the concept of reincarnation became a rare exception. Consideration of the soul within the most popular religions of the West involves the soul residing statically for eternity either in some type of heaven or hell at the death of the physical body. On the other hand, Eastern religions today still tend to promote the idea of reincarnation.

Reincarnation concepts themselves fundamentally encourage collectivism over individualism. If the MOS is oriented toward concepts of reincarnation, the population is likewise oriented toward valuing the group more than the individual. This is the rational conclusion based on the premise that if the individual soul has but one chance to harmonize with the Godhead, the soul should focus on itself, not another. If that same soul had multiple chances to "get it right," then the individual soul would be slightly less self-interested. Belief systems and religions specific to India and most of China accept concepts of reincarnation that fit very nicely within their specific MOS.

In Eastern thought, there are concepts that are completely alien to most Westerners today. Considerations of dharma, a type of cosmic order, and karma, the individual's personal record of moral account that is attached to the individual soul, are not reflected in Abrahamic religions. Some scholars would vehemently disagree with that statement and point to fundamental aspects of Judeo-Christian theology that seem to rephrase the exact concepts of dharma (God of Abraham) and karma (individual soul).

To that I would say that given the fact Eastern philosophy fundamentally resists the binds of a limiting overarching dogma, I doubt that Judeo-Christian ideas can be directly sourced to the same concepts which birthed Jainism and Buddhism.

With contrary opinions acknowledged, I suggest that Eastern philosophy is different. Hindu societies common on the Indian subcontinent instruct citizens that a primary responsibility of the individual is to consider how his or her personal actions impact universal dharma. To negatively impact dharma is to work against the wishes of the God Brahma. The individual must make these personal sacrifices to benefit the group, which in turn pleases God.

The Hindu religion, which originated from Eastern philosophy, advocates sacrifice of personal desires for the good of the group, which in turn pleases God and ultimately helps improve the odds that the individual soul will be reincarnated into a better life than the former. In contrast, the Christian religion, an evolution of Judaism under Western philosophical influence, advocates mimicry of Jesus as the ultimate version of a self-sacrificing human. In both religions, self-sacrifice is encouraged to aid the individual soul, but the reincarnation concept makes the Hindu dogma slightly less severe than the Christian dogma. Certainly, being reincarnated to a lower life-form due to a failure of the soul is bad, but not quite as bad as eternal damnation as promoted by the Christian faith. Despite these differences regarding the fate of the soul, we should note that both religious philosophies emphasize personal sacrifice to the benefit of the soul.

Philosophies of the Godhead can be to some extent traced to cultures going back at least five thousand years. From those origins, specific Ultrathoughts evolved and eventually came to define regional distinctions in philosophies. Today we might consider that Eastern philosophy is more closely aligned with man's fundamental or innate mindset if we assume concepts of world soul are essential to the mind of man. It is possible that this base or core theory of the Godhead is remarkably similar to Eastern philosophy even as it is expressed today, but there is no way to confirm this line of ultra-thinking. Though we have indications of what very ancient cultures thought, there are no written records going back beyond roughly 2,500–3,000 years.

In further consideration of religion and the MOS, let's think beyond concepts of God and consider political structures. The MOS is comprised of values and within those values are consideration of God and governance. Even if a society has adopted the concept of separation of church and state, the MOS inherently maintains some concept of what is expected of a worthy government. A political philosophy that is not in harmony with the society's dominant religious philosophy will create stresses in the MOS. If a religious philosophy elevates the value of the collective, one would assume the political leadership is expected to do the same. For example, if the MOS and dominant religious belief accept racism or a caste system, the government would be expected to do the same. When considering religion, we generally note this exact result. Governments are harmonized within the context of their society's dominant spiritual philosophies. Societies that value collectivism governed under a philosophy of socialism and communism fit keenly with philosophies of the East. Societies in the West, particularly that of the United States, value the liberty of the individual more than those of the East, and in doing so promote a more laissez-faire style of government.

As our culture further evolves into a truly global society, we should immediately recognize a problem. Attempting to integrate a population of people who have two entirely different views of God, soul, and government will create problems, unless one or both populations compromise their core beliefs. Any society which functions as a theocracy has intermingled God and government within its understanding of reality. These citizens aren't going to simply flip to accept a government that fails to recognize their historical view of God within such context. Naturally, the inverse is also true. A secular population won't accept a government which overtly demands recognition of a particular Godhead design, when the government heretofore has favored none. A failure to synchronize all three—religion, politics, and MOS—will risk destroying the society.

Conflicts of this nature have been obvious recently as we've watched societies fail because outsiders promoted a system of government that was not harmonized with spiritual beliefs and the MOS. Historically, the script has been reversed; societies failed when outsiders promoted religions that ran contra to the politics. Regardless of the modus operandi, when one ponders Ultrathoughts regarding a religion that is foreign to the thinker, it is important to consider that religion often means far more than concerns of spiritual and religious dogma. Local government is tied in one degree or another to its local spiritual beliefs.

After considering the overall dynamic, let's bring our discussion forward to specifically consider Western society and how its overt separation of church and state has led to challenges regarding globalization. Western societies over the past few hundred years have been the most economically prosperous. As a result, it appears reasonable to promote the political and economic structure globally. But now that we have a basic understanding of the influence religious beliefs have on the MOS and the need to synchronize philosophies, we note a logical flaw if the Western model is promoted across the globe.

Separation of church and state exists in harmony with most Christian societies and owes its conceptual origin to reformed Christians of the 1550s. Christian thinkers were instrumental during this period and over time influenced the MOS. Now, hundreds of years later, the concept of separation has begun to evolve into secularization, meaning the MOS is beginning to express inertia that shuns spiritual concepts completely. What would be the result if a largely secularized Europe and the United States came to invite integration of individuals who do not share a value system that appreciates not only separation of church and state but complete secularization of society? Clearly, something would need to change; either the government would need to adopt laws in harmony with the spiritual religion of the new citizens, or the new citizens would need to compromise their spiritual beliefs. A failure to recognize this inevitability is apparent to many. Regardless of why the problem is being ignored, the result is playing out before our eyes.

In summary, any ultra-thinking concerning religion is likely to become extremely complicated and without significant effort may lead to fundamentally flawed Ultrathoughts. Due to the very nature of this topic, the thinker must consider the philosophical origin of the religion, the MOS of the culture in which the believer is immersed, and whether the religion is intertwined with the government. Without first devoting some time to these questions, there is little hope of developing a quality Ultrathought concerning differences between religions.

CHAPTER 21

RELIGIONS CAN BE NEUTRAL; WE SHOULDN'T BE

Religions are purely a construct of people and don't determine the fate of the soul. Being creations of human beings, religions—all of them—are anti-God. They are anti-God within the strict context of a philosophical discussion because they present a force of resistance to the Godhead. To say anti-God is not meant to imply religions are evil or wrong. Many, if not most, religions are quite beneficial because we live in a society. If we had no society—say it was just Adam and Eve living in paradise— there would be no need for the structure of any religion. Since we have billions of pairs of Adam and Eve on our planet, certainly our humanity can benefit from any number of religions.

Religions often promote beneficial rules, structure, and moral behavior to the benefit of humanity. They also help individuals maintain a sense of spiritual awareness. In our secular society we note they can be more like a social club, not really projecting any particular set of Godhead beliefs. Personally, I'm not sure these types of religions do much to help the soul of an individual but I won't say they are bad or somehow evil. Though, I will say that if they delude people in to thinking a social club membership will somehow benefit the soul, well, that wouldn't be good. Clubs are clubs. Religions can be clubs, but a worthy religion for the benefit of the soul is something more.

The worthiness of a religion is determined by whether its core philosophy provides a spiritual benefit to the soul of the individual. A worthy religion will also have a kind of harmony with the universe, while a flawed religion will not. A flawed religion is one that advances ideas that promote the destruction of the physical individual, the person, or the cosmos. Ideas that elevate the material world over the meta self we create is a promotion of the destruction of the person, so the religion of science is inherently wrong.

"Harmony with the universe" may strike you as a nebulous phrase, but I simply know of no other way to express this line of ultra-thinking. To be in harmony would mean to be in balance, unanimity, or accord. I can't help but recall the ancient philosopher Pythagoras; he probably used a similar description in his attempts to describe the inherent goodness of the cosmos. In this context, I speak of the Godhead in representation of pure love. For instance, to destroy, to kill, to ruin would not be in harmony with the universe as these are not only anti-God but offensive to our God-given sense of morality. In a strict sense, to build, to act, and to influence may also be considered anti-God, although they are not fundamentally negative or immoral. Given my view of reality, I consider an action done with noble intent to be a worthwhile act provided it is done with a pure heart and doesn't put an unnecessary burden upon anyone. In my mind-myth, a religion valuable to the individual, group, or physical matter of the universe would be one based on love. Such a religion would not be offensive to the overall sensibilities of mankind but could still, on occasion, run counter to the benefit of the collective group.

This point has a certain nuance: religion can be beneficial to an individual and detrimental to the group or vice versa. For example, a specific religion might mandate a day of rest for the individual. If an individual, say a farmer, took a day of rest, that's one less day of food production for the collective group. The day of rest benefitted the individual but not the group. Of course, in all but the most extreme circumstances, one day makes little difference. Therefore, we can say that in this specific example our religion is not in violation of our sensibilities.

Let's now consider a rather common religious belief of old that required the sacrifice of a clear-minded, yet physically incapable, individual. In this case, the good of the group is elevated above the individual. Does that mean the entire religion is offensive? What if that individual person seeks relief from his or her mortal existence? In my philosophy, a tenant of a religion that promotes the destruction of an individual is an afront to the Godhead, period. Whether or not the individual should be killed is not the prerogative of our peers. Is it the prerogative of the person? That is a question to be answered only by the person in question, not by you or me.

Any religion that creates a dense myth that elevates the material realm, the group, or the individual to a status that denigrates the spiritual essence of any other living being, obviously doesn't promote the love of the Godhead. Likewise, one should accept the fact that religions tend to be bound regionally, culturally, and to an era of time. Religions, to a very large extent, evolve to be in harmony within the culture dominated by their own unique MOS. The MOS, too, comes to evolve within these dynamics. When considering the faith and religious practice of another, extreme caution should be used. Still, we are blessed with a mind. We can use that mind to ultra-think whether or not foreign beliefs can be reconciled to certain fundamental truths of the universe.

Your story develops within your culture. Personal concepts of the Godhead within the mind grow while considering the importance of the MOS, friends, and family. An individual who undertakes a spiritual quest in reconsideration of their impressions of the Godhead risks compromising spiritual concepts of the mind entirely. Why? Because of the inertia of the MOS.

Your society is constantly influencing your mind-myth. Therefore, your own culture's dominant philosophy of the Godhead, and even its dominant religion, probably fits you best. Things simply evolved that way. Change your narrative or strip it bare without appreciating the MOS, and you again risk conflict with your group. This is the primary reason ultra-thinking religion is very challenging.

Put plainly, in ultra-thinking religion you will overtly reject your religious indoctrination in hopes of bringing forth spiritual clarity. While rejection is part of the process, rejection of existing belief is not necessarily permanent. Still, it is a high-risk proposition. What if you get the first part right, and you succeed in rejecting the family religion only to find you don't devote enough time into rebuilding an improved spiritual belief? That is an incredibly common occurrence in the lives of Western individuals. People reject their heritage, family values, and historical religion, but fail to prioritize their newly-liberated mind. They then become spiritually neutral, basically agnostics.

Admittedly in the previous sections, I did generally praise the state of an agnostic. In fact, I went so far as to speculate that the agnostic may be preferred by the Godhead. Still, if you understood my earlier point, you'll recall the agnostic described was not disinterested or distracted, but simply confused. When an agnostic becomes truly neutral in their opinion of God, eventually their feeble attempt to "keep God alive" within mind-myth will fail. So, the distinction is that confusion and doubt are fine, but indifference is not.

Ultra-thinking your personal religion can be like jumping out of a plane without a parachute, hoping a buddy will grab you before you fall. As you strip religious dogma from your mind-myth you risk losing your fundamental Godhead beliefs in the process. I managed to survive my jump but you are warned. Don't simply assume you can rebuild spiritual belief in a productive manner without a tremendous amount of time and effort. If you are content with your religion, you're happy and well-adjusted maybe it makes more sense to not ultra-think religion.

CHAPTER 22

CHAPTER 22

JUST TO BE PERFECTLY CLEAR

Ultra-thinking the Godhead and religion worked for me, but it took years to happen. Like more than a few of my readers, I truly resented having been brought up in the Christian faith. Though I was respectful to my heritage I couldn't quite buy-in. I reasoned it would have been easier for me to ultra-think the Godhead without my foundational beliefs. Resentful of my self-created drama, I raised my children in a secular household. In hopes of justifying my actions and relieving my own cognitive dissidence, I concluded that if my own children ever chose to seek God at least they'd start from a blank slate. Reflecting on that child-rearing decision today, I still have mixed emotions.

My path in ultra-thinking God was painful, to say the least. Looking back, I suspect that I deeply wanted to shed any and all Godhead beliefs because such meta concepts run fundamentally against the leaning of my brain. This attempt to lose God was wrapped in a quest to explain. Being raised in a homogenous and rather rigid segment of the Bible Belt region I was taught that once I had abandoned my faith, I would not seek to rebuild anything. You might say I was more of a loser than a seeker. Logically, once my faith was officially lost, I'd find comfort in a modern materialistic world, never think of God again and live happily ever after.

To my complete shock, after ultra-thinking the Godhead, what I ultimately discovered was that the earliest themes of Christian philosophy made the most sense to me personally. These beliefs of my upbringing started to seem plausible when comprehended philosophically rather than in a physical sense. I became a believer in my God. Not through indoctrination, going to any church, or even the research that so fascinated me—I came to faith through my own indirect kind of prayer; a unique version of ultra-thinking.

What started as a quest to make sense of God morphed into a quest for enlightenment once I finally understood that the God-head defies explanation. Today, I see Jesus the Christ, the Holy Spirit, and the God of Abraham (The Holy Trinity) as being the Godhead. As a man Jesus somehow presented a physical presence of God. He was an actual person, a carpenter and rabbi who was murdered by the Romans.

Acknowledging the potential confusion that may come from my attempt to put this into words: Jesus as a living, breathing man was representative of God, just as a Temple was to the ancient Jews and a statue of Horus was to the dynastic Egyptians. The man—his essence—was God. As a believer who accepts guidance offered through the Holy Spirit of God, I am therefore *one* with God, in a manner similar to how ancient Jewish people became *one* with God through worship and sacrifice. Jesus is the Temple, the statue, The God.

My individual soul is timeless and temporarily partners with the body. This soul was pure but became contaminated at birth because the body allowed the soul to obtain a degree of separation from the meta presence of God. Care of soul is my responsibility. I owe a duty to God, and in expression of brotherly love to humanity I shall attempt to tend my soul with great care. While this is accomplished, my soul is in a heavenly state. At my earthly passing the fate of the soul is left to God.

Regarding the question of the resurrection of the man Jesus, a belief associated with Christianity, my view is equally clear in my mind today, but possibly challenging to write. As a common man of my era living in a modern mechanized world, I deem such an event plausible but still rather unlikely. Though a resurrection is unlikely I am saying, yes, there is a chance. This is an enlightened view because I gave it some ultra-thinking. I understand that science proves nothing, and I have an understanding of quantum mechanics. Just as a car can appear in your kitchen, there is a chance a mortal man literally walked and talked, being totally indistinguishable from any other human after he had been brutally crucified on a wooden cross one sunny day in Jerusalem. It is extremely unlikely that this is a physical truth, but it is not impossible. Therefore, since a physical reality can't bind the spiritual, I am at liberty to elect my belief in the resurrection.

With regard to prayer, here's the way I see things. A worthy prayer for another is potentially very important. I believe prayer works because I can influence metaphysical forces which are not understandable by human beings. Again, I find a hint of validation in this belief through my basic understanding of quantum mechanics. My prayer has the power to influence the life of another being through inexplicable forces of the cosmos.

Prayer also has a benefit to my person, my soul, if you will. Still, the only prayer beneficial for my individual soul is an anonymous prayer given for a person I shall never meet. My theory rests on this key point: If I pray for a friend and said prayer succeeds, I am personally pleased when I become aware of the result. I suggest this may indicate I have, in some small way taken ownership of said success. My ego is then inflated. To pray for an anonymous person means I shall never know of the success of my prayer. Any glory related to my effort remains with God because my ego has not been alerted of the success. This is the only way to help humanity while keeping my ego in check. In my faith, personal humility is key. I must constantly seek to deny ego any credit, so I can't pray for myself or anything that would remotely benefit me.

The only way to effectively meet all of my goals (glorify God, help humanity, and enrich my soul) is to seriously attempt to do what is right, spread brotherly love. This Ultrathought of a spiritual nature rests on the ideas of brotherly love and suppression of ego each exhibited by the model of Jesus of Nazareth. To express brotherly love is to love another as God does human beings. All of us are equal before God, so each person is infinitely important. Given my era, the location on the planet that my body became manifest, and my current interactions within Western society, he is all I personally need, although I suspect he is not the only model offered in representation of the universal Godhead. For that reason, I don't subscribe to the idea that my God is crucial to your own soul.

You may choose to consider my beliefs as you wish, but what I am is a believer in a Trinitarian philosophy that is generally the same one used as a basis for various sects of the Christian religion. Because I don't elevate Christian religion over the philosophy I don't subscribe to any creeds other than those of my own mind. Mine is a belief in the process of being and staying near the Godhead, interpreted by me as the One God of Abraham. My belief is bolstered but certainly not proven by my ultra-thinking regarding the very bizarre nature of the quantum. All of those strange notions I've previously spoken of in some way usually come back to some aspect of the spiritual realm. I ultra-think that these "hints" of the spiritual are meant for me, as they allow me to add credence to the "spiritual chapter" of my own mind-myth narrative.

Let me summarize my belief in a more philosophical tone for posterity:

Through the inexplicable workings of God, Jesus of Nazareth, came to manifest a person who serves as a type of bridge between the spiritual and physical realms. The Godhead sacrificed God Himself in this individual. God as the physical man—Jesus—epitomized self-sacrifice in representation of the brotherly love of the God. The resurrection of that same physical man, Jesus, who then became Jesus the Christ, further represented the conquest of the spiritual realm over all that is the physical reality of death.

Although the story of Jesus has a literal foundation, the nuance of the story - his ministry, life and resurrection - has evolved to become a tail rich in allegory. With that said, given the subject matter, neither the story nor any variation in the details can be proven an absolute impossibility. Though I'm absolutely certain the man existed, I can allow myself to have occasional doubts regarding my own philosophy. In times of doubt, I shall simply hope to believe tomorrow because I know *hope creates faith, and faith does not disappoint* (Google that one).

If you research ancient beliefs, you will find a particularly common theme: *The spiritual begets physical (meta creates a reality in the mind) which in turn cedes its place in deference to the spiritual in the end (physical reality bows to the powers of the meta).* A belief in allegory can create a 'literal' truth of the mind. That is what it means to have faith in God and cultivate a proper mortal life which benefits the immortal soul. Believe in the Godhead, believe in the journey, and you have your truth. You will manifest the God in which you believe. Believe in none, receive apathy from the Godhead in return.

I'm confident Jesus lived, taught, and provided an example for humanity. For what purpose, I will never be absolutely sure. I choose to believe he truly became one with the Godhead. When the person was shown to defy death, God provided an example for humanity: brotherly love embodied. This is likely just one of multiple examples of the power of God, but it is the only one of personal relevance to me. The larger point here is that the physical doesn't matter to me in the end. Only a consistent focus on such love offered by the Godhead can keep my soul pure (i.e. in heaven). Consistently fail in mission, lose focus, lose faith in God, and I will damn my soul. Whether this description has any relevance to any other person on the planet makes no difference.

My personal insights and my own narrative of God are unique to me. In casual conversation, I prefer not to speak of my version of God to those who have a strong spiritual mind of their own unless we enter the discussion with an understanding: we're purely discussing philosophy. In this book, that is exactly what we are doing. If you're a stalwart believer, I suggest you don't even bother to give my views a second thought. If you are a seeker of spiritual truth, I hope my convoluted truth gives you confidence to seek your own. You probably would do no worse than I. If, in your own opinion, my freedom from dogma disqualifies me from claiming Christianity as my faith, I respect the point and move on unfazed. Frankly, until I did some ultra-thinking, I would have thought the same.

CONCLUSION

I wrote this series at the urging of my daughter, Adrianne, who said she was overwhelmed by my random Ultrathought dissertations on anthropology, quantum mechanics, reality, and God. She asked that I "write that stuff down." Being a left-brainer, I had little interest in writing a published work let alone a trilogy, particularly when some of "that stuff" might be viewed as controversial or even offensive. While I love friendly debate and even an occasional argument, as I get older it seems that most debates tend to morph into personal attacks after about ten minutes. My sisters are proof of that point.

I hate confrontation, don't mind being a peacemaker, and have no desire to be the advocate for my forbidden philosophy. Yet, gazing at a photo of my daughter's first child, Grace, I started to wonder if I'd ever even live to share "my pearls of wisdom" with that little girl as I had done with my daughter. Then I recalled that I never did have that one last row with my own father and never was certain he died believing the very literal interpretation of God he had professed when I was a young boy. My sisters and I debate that issue to this day. I wish he would have written "that stuff" down.

Before starting this work, I needed to ultra-think the true purpose of sharing my ideas. If I truly believe we all live our own delusion, why bother? Why should it matter what anyone ultra-thinks, let alone an ordinary guy like me? Furthermore, why put in the effort to publish a book when a simple journal would suffice? Then it hit me.

What is worth sharing to that little girl and indeed humanity are not my specific Ultrathoughts, which continue to evolve, but the process of ultra-thinking combined with encouragement to keep her mind vibrant. There's no doubt that one's personal delusion can be improved through intentional thought. I have gained clarity and am doing a much better job of respecting those who disagree with me. From ultra-thinking I've learned the same absolute truth that Plato taught eons ago: to think is good.

Ultrathoughts Tripartite contains words of encouragement wrapped around an illusion of my mind. In jest and with optimism, I call it my poetry. The goal here has been to present a fearless advocation for the creation of deeply contemplative thoughts for the benefit of humanity by providing examples of Ultrathoughts. Such examples drive home the point that thinking people don't always agree, and dogma, whether of science or spiritual religion, doesn't provide definitive answers. By becoming consciously aware of our own left- or right-brain thought filter, and actively suppressing its influence we can derive better answers from the mind. Better answers to life's questions build an ever-improving mind-myth that in turn results in a healthy state of being for both the individual and humanity. That, in a nutshell, is why I advocate for ultra-thinking in the production of Ultrathoughts.

I first explained the concept of ultra-thinking to my Postmodern Society professor decades ago. I even wrote a paper on the concept. The paper was called "Ultra-thinking: If thoughts are linear, then more thoughts faster lead to better solutions sooner." At that point, I had no awareness of my own ideology. I was attempting to explain that if answers were the product of mental calculations the faster knowledge could be digested by the mind, the greater the advantage to the thinker—perfectly reasonable assumptions penned by an ideologically immersed left-brainer.

Upon reflection today, it's seems I was making a case for Red Bull energy drink. The professor gave me the impression that he thought I had a screw loose. Now that I recall, he called me "obsessive," just like my sisters. Regardless, I received an A in the class. I suppose only a left-brainer would bother to mention the grade . . . my struggles will continue.

Hopefully you have enjoyed our journey regarding the mind and have a new process to enhance your narrative. Maybe you will contemplate various subjects, including your existence on this wondrous planet and the potential for more beyond. If you want to put your own Ultrathoughts to pen or the web, contact us at *www.ultrathoughts.com*, and maybe we can help you be a visionary rather than a victimized thinker.

Let me leave you with an Ultrathought by the most courageous ultra-thinker of history:

"We can easily forgive a child who is afraid of the dark;
the real tragedy of life is when people are afraid of the light."
Plato

EPILOGUE TO THE ULTRATHOUGHTS TRIPARTITE

My heartfelt thanks go out to everyone who took the time to suffer through a reading of any early drafts of the series. These specific individuals have been instrumental in production of the vision: Ed Bowers, Ilil Arbel, Jonathan Wallach, Angel Jimenez, Mariana Taramasco, Lynn Andrews, Julina Small, Joshua Reish, Jessica Houdart, Berge Design, and the folks at Bublish.com. Special thanks goes out to my wife, Corinne. She not only put-up with my 'secondjob' for well over a year, she has to listen to stuff like this every day from a nut like me.

During the process of writing, I floated several manuscripts among friends and publishers. As you might expect, some liked it, some didn't. There were a number of important suggestions and criticisms. If you recall, I'm a middle child with two sisters. One thinks from the left like me and the other is a right-brain-leaning more creative type of person. The creative one, of course, offered to help. The older one refused to even read a draft. I think her exact words were, "Oh brother, that's stupid." I laugh because my father would have had a very similar reaction, at least until he had heard I called his view of the truth a delusion. Then he would have threatened to disown me if I dared to publish!

Regardless of the number of rewrites, I pressed on for over a year, all the while running my business. I did so because once I told my daughter I would write a book it became an obsession, like finishing the remodeling of a house by a given date, completing fifty half marathons, or collecting one example of every Honda model CT70 motorcycle ever released in the United States (see my personal Honda museum at *www.trail70.com*). Since obsession guides most of my activities, once I decided to take on this project, come hell or high water, these books were going to be written.

Along the way, more than one publisher expressed interest and even money in exchange for publishing rights. If you know anything about the industry, you understand publishers need to control the product. That makes sense to me. In fact, it makes dollars and cents for them and the author. Still, being the person I am, the loss of control was simply unacceptable. So I decided to self-publish despite having no idea what I was doing. Though I'm no expert, reach out to me if you want my insight into the process of self-publishing on Amazon.

I bring all this up for a reason. Self-publishing your ideas, your ideas derived through ultra-thinking, is something you should consider. When you publish you can get an ISBN and Library of Congress Catalog number (LCCN). These facilitate the indexing of your book. Given the fact that your work is then part of a timeless index, your words will become cataloged for history. While your blog, college paper, or simple social media posts will probably never be adequately indexed anytime soon, with these numbers you're not only an author, but you may be a source for your legacy.

Have no fear, go on record with your own Ultrathoughts! Even if my sister will call you stupid for choosing to write, maybe your great-great-granddaughter one hundred years from now won't.

GLOSSARY FOR FULL SERIES

collective mind (CM): Similar to *mind of society* as a societal attitude, belief, tone, style, and sensibility; a meta idea that does act with intent. Comparable to the idea of a *world soul* having a presence and/or relationship to the Godhead.

complex (dynamic) system: A system composed of many components that may interact with each other. Aggregate activity is nonlinear (not derivable from the summations of the activity of individual components), adaptive, and open. Variability is seen as an inherent property of the system although it typically exhibits a hierarchical self-organization under certain pressures.

dogma: A set of principles laid down by an authority and perpetuated by perception of dominance. A code of tenets or body of doctrine.

epigenetic: Relating to nongenetic influences on gene expression. A general term used to describe dynamics not fully understood by scientists in the field of genetics.

god/God: Superhuman presence, being, or force. Brahma, Zeus, Jesus the Christ, God of Abraham, and simply "God" are among various names used to describe a superhuman presence.

Godhead: A generalized or meta concept of God. The domain or realm of all that is godlike.

ideology: Your ideas wrapped around your personal mind-myth narrative.

indoctrination: The process of teaching someone ideas and standards with or without intent.

hard science: Often associated with the natural sciences; biology, chemistry, physics. Sciences associated with a well-defined methodological rigor.

Hellenist: A person speaking the Greek language whose outlook and way of life was significantly influenced by the Greek Empire of ancient times, regardless of heritage or geographic location.

Hellenistic era: Defined by Wikipedia.org as being from 323 BCE to 31 BCE, although dates assigned by other sources vary.

meta: Non-material, unknown, or spiritual.

metaphysical: See *meta*.

mind: Your ideas and concepts. Not quite so defined as to be a story, but similar.

mind-myth, narrative, personal story: The way you think. Your ideas woven into a metaphorical story that serves as a framework from which you perceive information.

mind of society (MOS): Societal attitude, shared beliefs, tone, style, and sensibility having no spiritual or physical presence other than the force of inertia. MOS is a meta idea that has no ability to act with intent.

monotheism: A belief in and associated worship of a specific and single God.

naturalism: see *religion of science*.

philosophy: Study and contemplation of the fundamental nature of knowledge, reality, and existence.

physical realm: The domain of reality dealing with the material substance of matter. Deals with the known or that which is deemed knowable.

polytheism: A belief in and associated worship of multiple gods.

quantum: Discrete quantity of energy. An expression used to describe a non-material presence of energy, momentum, or electric charge.

realm: Domain, area, kingdom.

religion: A belief in and associated worship of a theme, set of ideas, or controlling presence.

religion (spiritual): A belief in and associated worship of a superhuman presence.

religion (non-spiritual): Beliefs and worship that are not associated with any superhuman presence.

religion of science: A belief in and associated worship of a set of ideas that deny any superhuman presence. Naturalism or Darwinism.

science: A systematic methodology that organizes knowledge in the form of a testable hypothesis (informed guess).

scientific method: The methodology that involves observation, cognitive assumption, mathematics, and specific testing in an attempt to disprove a hypothesis.

soft science: Often associated with social sciences; economics, philosophy, sociology, psychology. Sciences ill-defined and less subject to a well-defined methodological rigor.

soul: A spiritual consideration that deals with the immaterial part of a being either human, other animal, and/or substance matter of life.

spiritual: The domain of belief, truth, or reality that deals with the immaterial, unknown, unknowable, and/or Godhead. All that is not within the physical realm.

ultra-thinking: An act of purposeful thinking in a manner that restrains personal ideology, indoctrinated belief, and existing expertise of the thinker as it forces the mind to actively seek outlandish new information.

Ultrathought: Deep contemplative thought, idea, or epiphany as a product of ultra-thinking.

world soul: A spiritual consideration that deals with the immaterial part of the cosmos, nature, universal consciousness, and self-awareness of a physical substance.

www.ingramcontent.com/pod-product-compliance
Lightning Source LLC
Chambersburg PA
CBHW021235090426
42740CB00006B/543